Financial Risk Management

Financial Risk Management

From Metrics to Human Conduct

FRANTZ MAURER

WILEY

This edition first published 2024

Frantz Maurer ©2024

The right of **Frantz Maurer** to be identified as the authors of this work has been asserted in accordance with law.

Registered Office(s)
John Wiley & Sons, Inc., 111 River Street, Hoboken, NJ 07030, USA
John Wiley & Sons Ltd, The Atrium, Southern Gate, Chichester, West Sussex, PO19 8SQ, UK

Editorial Office
The Atrium, Southern Gate, Chichester, West Sussex, PO19 8SQ, UK

For details of our global editorial offices, customer services, and more information about Wiley products visit us at www.wiley.com

Wiley also publishes its books in a variety of electronic formats and by print-on- demand. Some content that appears in standard print versions of this book may not be available in other formats. Designations used by companies to distinguish their products are often claimed as trademarks. All brand names and product names used in this book are trade names, service marks, trademarks or registered trademarks of their respective owners. The publisher is not associated with any product or vendor mentioned in this book.

Library of Congress Cataloging-in-Publication Data is Available:

ISBN 9781119885290 (Cloth)
ISBN 9781119885306 (ePDF)
ISBN 9781119885313 (ePub)

Cover Design: Wiley
Cover Image: © Oxygen/Getty Images

SKY10062108_120723

Brief Contents

Foreword

Writing a foreword or a preface for a book is always a great honour, a sign of recognition and a wonderful pleasure. Writing a foreword for Frantz Maurer's book is even more than that for me, for several reasons.

The first is that I have known Frantz for more than 30 years. I was a member of his PhD committee and was impressed by the quality of his research and the content of his doctoral thesis. I followed his career afterwards and got a full confirmation of his intellectual and analytical ability, his passion and enthusiasm for the field of finance in general, and the risk management segment in particular. We worked together in some executive programmes and published together, in 2006, a widely used Harvard Business School note: "Understanding corporate-value-at-risk through a comprehensive and simple example".

In his teaching and consulting activities, Frantz has always demonstrated a perfect combination of theory and practice, reflection and action, strategic skills and operational capabilities. His high integrity and very solid values, together with his motivation, taste for hard work and desire to share knowledge and experience, have constantly been recognized in the academic and business worlds.

The second reason is obviously closely correlated with the previous one. When Wiley asked me to write a book on Financial Risk Management, my immediate reaction was to associate Frantz with the project. We decided to co-author it and had long and fruitful discussions on its objectives, content and target readership. Unfortunately, severe health problems on my side forced me to significantly reduce my work pressure and made it impossible for me to continue this initial common project. I left Frantz in charge of the whole book and, despite a very heavy academic schedule, he was able to deliver a very good product.

The third reason is related to the content of the book. The recent financial disasters and wrongdoings in the banking and financial industry have shown that traditional commonly used risk indicators and measures, even if they remain useful, are too often inefficient to predict and prevent these disasters and that traditional actions are, most of the time, unable to avoid their repetition. "*Virtue cannot be regulated. Even the strongest supervision cannot guarantee good conduct.*" This comment by Mark Carney, a former governor of the Bank of England, was made in 2011 and, despite this warning, in the last 10 years, more than two-thirds of banks' operational losses have been connected to misconduct, which damages public trust in the banking and financial sector and may strongly contribute to systemic instability. As Frantz Maurer rightly shows, the Holy Grail of financial risk management should shift from pure quantitative risk metrics to the monitoring of human behaviours and the creation of a conduct risk culture, contributing to significantly reduce dangerous practices in financial institutions. It is not just about the figures!! It is about appropriate behaviours and good conduct. Financial risk management is in the process of entering a new era, moving from an excessive reliance on a purely financial quantitative approach to a greater emphasis on misconduct and misbehaviour in the business sphere, ultimately putting it on a more solid cultural basis.

Marc BERTONECHE

Emeritus Chair Professor of Management, University of Bordeaux

Former Visiting Professor, Harvard Business School

Associate Fellow, University of Oxford

Distinguished Visiting Professor, HEC Paris

Acknowledgements

Obviously, the list of those who deserve my gratitude is extensive and far-reaching. Going to the origin, I wish to salute my friend Marc Bertoneche who generously shared with me the project of this book, offered by Wiley, which he had to give up for health issues. His support has been unwavering since my PhD.

I am also grateful to Thierry Roncalli, Head of Quant Portfolio Strategy at Amundi Asset Management, for his help each time I had issues with GAUSS coding. Part II of this textbook and the toy examples dealing with banking regulation are highly inspired by the materials he developed.

I also thank Pierre Pourquery, Partner at EY and Head of Capital Markets, and Helyette Geman, Research Professor at Johns Hopkins University and 'Financial Engineer of the Year 2022', for having initiated a fruitful collaboration about conduct risk. I have benefited from the high level of their knowledge and unique professional experience.

List of Acronyms and Symbols

Acronyms

AMA	Advanced Measurement Approach
ASF	Available Stable Funding
AT1	Additional Tier 1
BCBS	Basel Committee on Banking Supervision
BIC	Bayesian Information Criterion
BIS	Bank for International Settlements
BL	Bill of Lading
BPCE	Banque Populaire Caisse d'Epargne
CAPM	Capital Asset Pricing Model
CB	Capital Conservation Buffer
CCB	Countercyclical Capital Buffer
cdf	cumulative distribution function
CEO	Chief Executive Officer
CET1	Common Equity Tier 1
CF_VaR	Cornish–Fisher Value-at-Risk
COCON	Code of Conduct
CRS	Conduct Risk Score
EAD	Exposure at Default
ECAI	External Credit Assessment Institution
EL	Expected Loss
EMEIA	Europe, the Middle East, India and Africa
ES	Expected Shortfall
EVT	Extreme Value Theory
EWMA	Exponentially Weighted Moving Average
ExCo	Executive Committee
EY	Ernst & Young Global Limited
FCA	Financial Conduct Authority
F&P	Fit and Proper individuals
FSB	Financial Stability Board
FX	Foreign Exchange market
GAFAM	Google (Alphabet), Apple, Facebook (Meta), Amazon and Microsoft

GARCH	Generalized Autoregressive Conditional Heteroscedasticity
GEV	Generalized Extreme Value
GBP	Great British Pound
GDPR	General Data Protection Regulation
G-SIB	Global Systemically Important Bank
HQLA	High-Quality Liquid Assets
HFT	High-Frequency Trading
HR	Human Resources
IRB	Internal Ratings-Based
KPI	Key Performance Indicator
KYC	Know Your Customer
LCR	Liquidity Coverage Ratio
LGD	Loss Given Default
M	Effective maturity
MD	Managing Director
NPC	National Payments Council
MDD	Maximum Drawdown
MtM	Mark-to-Market
NBFI	Non-Bank Financial Intermediation
NSFR	Net Stable Funding Ratio
OBS	Off-Balance Sheet
OECD	Organization for Economic Cooperation and Development
PD	Probability of Default
pdf	probability density function
P&L	Profit and Loss
PPI	Payment Protection Insurance
PRA	Prudential Regulation Authority
RSF	Required Stable Funding
SEC	Securities Exchange Commission
SFT	Securities Financing Transactions
SM&CR	Senior Managers and Certification Regime
SMF	Senior Management Function
RW	Risk Weight
RWA	Risk-Weighted Asset
T-Bills	Treasury Bills
VaR	Value-at-Risk
VBA	Visual Basic for Applications
VCM	Variance–Covariance Matrix
VP	Vice President

Symbols

α	confidence level
$\mathbb{C}$	required capital charge
CM^-	negative (or bad) conduct markers
CM^+	positive (or good) conduct markers
$\mathbb{C}_{MR}$	market risk capital
$\mathbb{C}_{OR}$	capital charge for operational risk
$\mathcal{D}$	probability distribution
∂	partial derivative
$\mathbb{E}[\ ]$	mathematical expectation
eK	excess kurtosis
ES_α^G	Gaussian Expected Shortfall at the confidence level α
ES_α^H	historical Expected Shortfall at the confidence level α
F	losses distribution
ξ	penalty coefficient
K	kurtosis
λ	decay factor
$\mathcal{L}(h)$	drawdown function
m_c	multiplication factor
mES_i	marginal Expected Shortfall of asset i
MtM_s	shocked MtM
$\mu(P\&L)$	expected return of P&L
$mVaR_i$	marginal Value-at-Risk of asset i
$\mathcal{N}(\mu,\sigma)$	Gaussian (or normal) distribution with mean μ and standard deviation σ
P_A	current price
$\phi(x)$	probability density function of the standardized Gaussian (or normal) distribution
$\Phi(x)$	cumulative density function of the standardized Gaussian (or normal) distribution
$\Phi^{-1}(\alpha)$	inverse of the standardized Gaussian (or normal) distribution
$P\&L_{i:n}$	ith-order statistic in a sample of n observations
$P\&L\uparrow$	P&L values sorted in ascending order
$P_{s,t}$	shocked price simulated at time t
P_t^i	price of asset i at time t
$\mathcal{R}$	recovery rate
$\dot{r}^i(t)$	standardized returns of asset i
R_t^i	return of asset i at time t
RC_i	risk contribution of asset i
$RC_i^\%$	risk decomposition of asset i expressed as a percentage
$\rho_{i,j}$	correlation coefficient between assets i and j

S	skewness
σ_{ij}	covariance between assets i and j
$\sigma(\text{P\&L})$	volatility of P&L
$\breve{t}^*$	return period (extreme)
$\breve{t}(x)$	return period
VaR_α^*	relative Value-at-Risk at the confidence level α
VaR_α^H	historical Value-at-Risk at the confidence level α
VaR_α^G	Gaussian Value-at-Risk at the confidence level α
VaR_α^{MC}	Monte-Carlo Value-at-Risk at the confidence level α
w_i	weight of asset i
z_{cf}^{VaR}	Cornish–Fisher scaling parameter

Introduction

There's a new boss in town and its name is conduct risk: failure to adequately assess and monitor the risks associated with highly risky strategies, practices contrary to the interests of clients, market collusion, regulatory reporting infractions, foreign currency rigging and money laundering. These are just some of the conduct breaches major banks worldwide have been fined for, and it is not over yet. Welcome to the amazing and worrisome world of misconduct in the banking industry!

In the past 10 years, around 70% of banks' operational losses have been connected to misconduct risk (also known as conduct risk). In its Global Risk 2021 report, the Boston Consulting Group mentions that in 2020, banks in Europe and North America paid $13 billion in penalties. Cumulative penalties since 2009 now total $394 billion. In February 2019, the Head of the International Monetary Fund (and Current Head of the European Central Bank), Christine Lagarde, warned: *"a decade on from the financial crisis, bad bankers have not learnt from the 2008 crash, with compensation levels reaching record highs on Wall Street and in other financial centers"*, and thus the financial industry needs an *"ethics upgrade"*.

What went wrong? This question is not easy to answer, but the idea that risk management should no longer be exclusively about developing complex mathematical models and equations is gaining momentum within major financial institutions. New approaches, perspectives and initiatives are required. This is not to say that the technical side of risk management must be put aside.[1] Risk metrics are still useful to quantify a potential loss for a given time horizon and confidence interval. Stated differently, Value-at-Risk, the expected shortfall and risk contributions calculation, has a rosy future. But risk management must go beyond financial risk metrics that are inefficient at identifying early warning signals of misconduct.

Despite the warning flags raised by the 2008 global financial turmoil, numerous occurrences of poor conduct and wrongdoing continue to take place within major financial institutions around the world. The underlying question raised by this book is: *Did purely financial risk management fail?* This question is deliberately provocative and somewhat counter-intuitive when it comes to writing a book dedicated to financial risk management and targeting, among others, risk practitioners working in financial institutions. The author intends to deviate from the mainstream approach. Instead of mainly relying on equations and mathematical models, he contends that financial risk management should benefit from integrating behavioural issues.

Financial risk management is now entering a new era, moving from an excessive reliance on a purely financial approach towards risk to greater emphasis on misconduct and misbehaviour in the business sphere, and ultimately a more solid grounding in improved firm culture. The financial side of risk management is now mature. A huge number of risk tools and models are available—from the simplest to the most sophisticated. From an academic standpoint, some risk measurement methods may appear to be old-fashioned. However, they are still used by professionals for different reasons: they may be more robust, easier to calibrate, but mainly speaking they are understandable and easy to implement.

Central to this book is not to reduce financial risk management to a quantitative approach, but to extend its scope to include behavioural and conduct issues that cut across the entire organization. Its objective is twofold:

1. Providing the reader with a survival toolbox of financial risk management. The aim is to explain how to express a risk exposure in terms of a potential loss. We explain why the two most widely used risk metrics— Value-at-Risk (VaR) and Expected Shortfall (ES)—are still useful, why they are seductive but dangerous and how to use them meaningfully.
2. Providing the reader with a refreshed approach towards risk management focusing on conduct risk. Here, the aim is to explain how to address poor conduct and misbehaviour in financial institutions. We develop a conduct risk index to benchmark the conduct performance of natural risk-takers like traders. This index measures how far risk-takers are from responsible behaviour.

The book is structured around these two dimensions and provides ready-to-use knowledge for anyone with an interest in financial risk management—particularly MBA students or their equivalent and senior executives, whatever the business they operate in. The book is not only dedicated to risk managers and, more generally, risk practitioners. It should also be helpful for anyone who may need to interact with a risk department within a company, be it financial or not.

The book is not a comprehensive review or catalogue of financial risk metrics and methods. The emphasis is put on those techniques that are used by professionals daily. Few quantitative skills are required to understand the different topics under review. The objective is to provide the reader with a ready-to-use (or almost) risk management toolbox to tackle real professional situations requiring risk analysis and decision-making. The book pivots away from the prevailing popular wisdom that financial risk management is purely mathematical and highly technical. This is even more valid for conduct risk—the new cornerstone of risk management.

Financial risk management is a wide field and this requires making choices about the topics to cover. The book does not encompass the different risks in **Figure 1**, but focuses on market risk because it is sufficiently operationalizable to allow a calculation to proceed towards a result. To put it differently, a solid background in mathematics, probability or statistics is not required to understand the methods depicted herein and duplicate the numerical applications.

Another choice is not to deal with portfolios of derivatives (mainly speaking, options) because their risk management is much more complicated than a portfolio of traditional assets such as, for example, equities (the simplest case). This complexity is mainly due to the non-linearity of these assets, resulting in non-linear exposures to risk factors. Such exposures are difficult to measure.

Let me illustrate this with a topical example. Let's say we are interested in measuring the market risk of a portfolio of equities (see **Figure 1**). The market risk factor of equities is the stock market price. If the stock price of my equities in the portfolio increases, this is a favourable outcome in terms of (market) risk because my portfolio value will increase, and the opposite if stock prices decrease. This is called linearity, and we say there is a linear relationship between the risk factor (stock price) and the portfolio exposure (the amount of money invested in equities). An increase in the former leads to an increase in the latter, and that holds true for the opposite pattern. Your exposure to the risk factor is linear and thus easy to measure.

Options tell a different story. The relationship between the option price and the underlying asset is not linear. This means that the price movement of the underlying asset (in our example, an equity) does not have a direct correlation with the option price. Another layer of complexity is that options are sensitive to parameters that are not always observable. A typical example is the volatility parameter. With the underlying asset, the implied volatility is the most important risk factor, but it is not a market price.

The book revolves around the concept of risk and it is structured into three parts:

- Part I. Navigating Banking Regulation
- Part II. The Financial Risk Management Landscape
- Part III. Getting Conduct Risk to Scale

NOTE

1. See Roncalli (2020) for a mathematical approach to financial risk management.

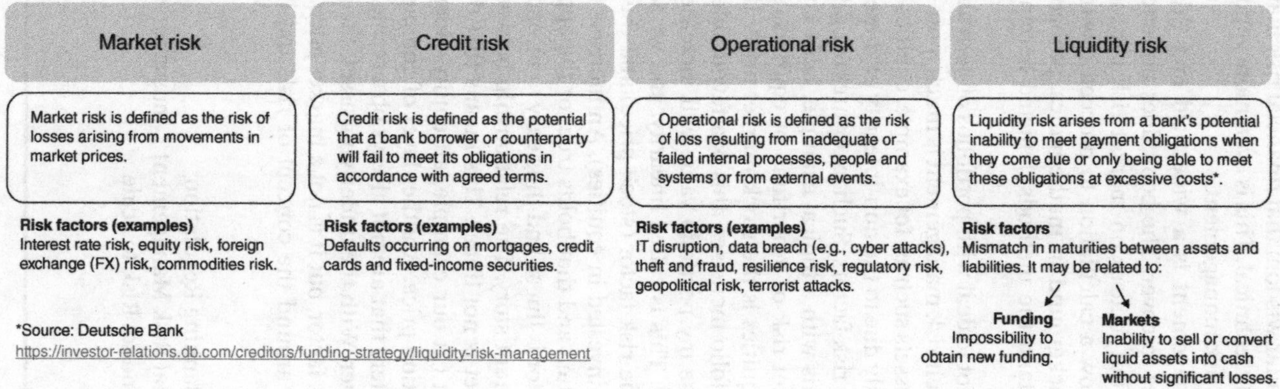
Market risk
Market risk is defined as the risk of losses arising from movements in market prices.
Risk factors (examples)
Interest rate risk, equity risk, foreign exchange (FX) risk, commodities risk.
Credit risk
Credit risk is defined as the potential that a bank borrower or counterparty will fail to meet its obligations in accordance with agreed terms.
Risk factors (examples)
Defaults occurring on mortgages, credit cards and fixed-income securities.
Operational risk
Operational risk is defined as the risk of loss resulting from inadequate or failed internal processes, people and systems or from external events.
Risk factors (examples)
IT disruption, data breach (e.g., cyber attacks), theft and fraud, resilience risk, regulatory risk, geopolitical risk, terrorist attacks.
Liquidity risk
Liquidity risk arises from a bank's potential inability to meet payment obligations when they come due or only being able to meet these obligations at excessive costs*.
Risk factors
Mismatch in maturities between assets and liabilities. It may be related to:
Funding
Impossibility to obtain new funding.
Markets
Inability to sell or convert liquid assets into cash without significant losses.
*Source: Deutsche Bank
https://investor-relations.db.com/creditors/funding-strategy/liquidity-risk-management

FIGURE 1 Financial risks in the banking industry

Financial Risk Management

One

Navigating Banking Regulation

In the aftermath of the failure of Herstatt Bank in Germany (in 1974), the central bank governors of the G10 established the Basel Committee—now named the Basel Committee on Banking Supervision (BCBS). It is the primary global standard setter for the prudential regulation of banks and provides a forum for regular cooperation on banking supervisory matters.[1] The Committee is headquartered at the Bank for International Settlements (BIS) in Basel, Switzerland. Its main objective is "[. . .] *to enhance financial stability by improving the quality of banking supervision worldwide, and to serve as a forum for regular cooperation between its member countries on banking supervision matters*".[2]

In this part, we stress what is essential for understanding the risk metrics and methods developed in the second part of the book. Knowing the alpha and omega of banking regulation is one way to develop skills and competencies in the field of banking risk management. We review the main milestones of the successive Basel frameworks, from Basel I to III, explaining how and why they have evolved over time. Finally, we address the regulatory viewpoint on climate-related financial risks.

NOTES

1. Its 45 members comprise central banks and bank supervisors from 28 jurisdictions.
2. Source: https://www.bis.org/bcbs/history.htm

## CHAPTER 1

A Brief History of the Basel Framework

Since its creation, the Basel Committee has set up international standards for bank regulations, specifically its three landmark updates which are commonly known as Basel I, Basel II and, more recently, Basel III, among multiple revisions.[1] The core idea behind this set of accords on capital adequacy requirements is to determine whether a bank possesses adequate reserves to deal with unexpected losses. In short, the Basel accords aim to provide a buffer against bank losses, protect creditors in the event of bank collapses and create disincentive for excessive risk-taking. The main milestones of banking supervision from 1988 to 2021 are displayed in **Figure 2**.

- **July 1988.** Publication of *International convergence of capital measurement and capital standards* (BCBS, 1988), commonly known as "The Basel Capital Accord" or Basel I. The standards in this document are mainly directed towards assessing capital in relation to credit risk (the risk of counterparty failure), the main risk incurred by most banks.
- **January 1996.** Publication of *Amendment to the capital accord to incorporate market risks* (BCBS, 1996). Banks will be required to measure and apply capital charges in respect to their market risks in addition to their credit risks.
- **June 2004.** Release of a revised capital framework generally known as Basel II. According to the Basel Committee: *"The new framework was designed to improve the way regulatory capital requirements reflect underlying risks and to better address the financial innovation that had occurred in recent years"*.
- **June 2006.** Implementation of the Basel II framework (BCBS, 2006).
- **July 2009.** Publication of *Revisions to the Basel II market risk framework* (BCBS, 2009). This text frequently refers to Basel 2.5 and provides an additional response to the 2007/09 financial turmoil. A salient feature of these revisions is the introduction of a stressed Value-at-Risk (VaR) requirement.

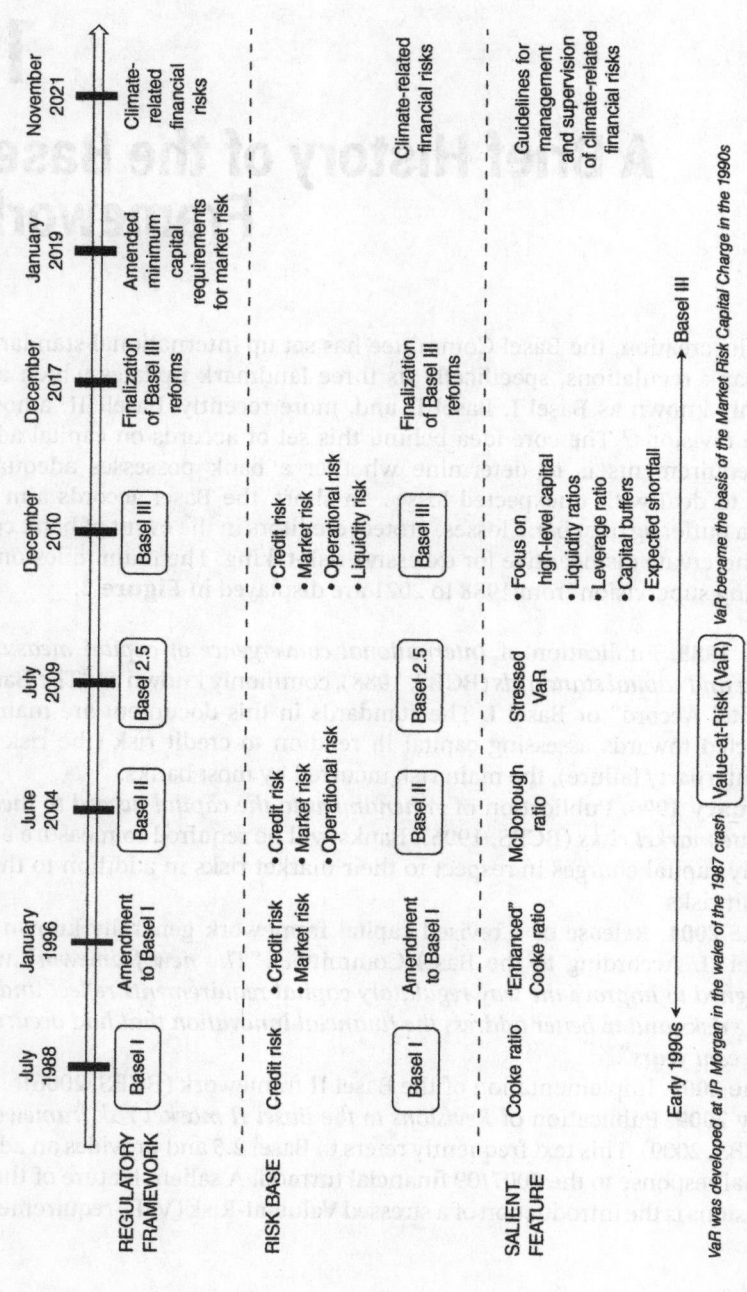

FIGURE 2 The key milestones of banking supervision

- **December 2010.** Publication of *Basel III: A global regulatory framework for more resilient banks and banking systems* (BCBS, 2010). According to this, *"the objective of the reforms is to improve the banking sector's ability to absorb shocks arising from financial and economic stress, whatever the source, thus reducing the risk of spillover from the financial sector to the real economy"*.
- **December 2017.** Finalization of Basel III reforms.
- **January 2019.** Publication of *Minimum capital requirements for market risk* (BCBS, 2019a). This document sets out the amended minimum capital requirements for market risk.
- **November 2021.** Publication of *Principles for the effective management and supervision of climate-related financial risks* (BCBS, 2021). This consultative document forms part of the Basel Committee's holistic approach to address climate-related financial risks within the banking sector.

In 2017, the Basel Committee agreed on fundamental changes for Basel III. Given the number of suggested changes (a mix of consultation papers and finalized standards), the Basel III reform was seen as a completely new framework, informally called Basel IV or Basel 3.1. Actually, the so-called Basel IV reform is the final version of Basel III, initially scheduled to begin implementation by 2015, and supposed to be fully implemented under transition rules by January 2025. As the deadline has been pushed back several times, it is still possible that it will be extended, although some provisions are already in place in some countries.

Recently, the Basel Committee disclosed its strategic priorities for 2023/24. The key themes include the following:[2]

- **Emerging risks and horizon scanning.** The Committee will perform a series of horizon-scanning exercises to analyse *"the impact of ongoing geopolitical developments, stagflationary dynamics, scaring effects and cross-border spillovers"*.
- **Digitalization of finance.** The Committee will publish a report on the on-going digitalization of finance, including hot topics such as the emergence of new entrants/suppliers in the banking system, the use of artificial intelligence and machine learning and big data, not to mention the prudential treatment of banks' cryptoasset exposures.
- **Climate-related financial risks.** The Committee will continue to address climate-related financial risks to the global banking system across the three dimensions of regulation, supervision and disclosure.
- **Monitoring and review of existing standards and guidance.** The Committee's work will be limited to a set of targeted initiatives, such as, but not limited to, an update to the core principles for effective banking

supervision, developing additional guidance with regard to banks' inter-connections with non-bank financial intermediation and reviewing the shock scenarios on interest rate risk in the banking book.

- **Implementation and evaluation.** The Committee will continue to evaluate the impact and efficacy of Basel III in the medium term.

NOTES

1. They are available on the website of the Bank for International Settlements (BIS): https://www.bis.org/bcbs/publications.htm
2. Source: https://www.bis.org/bcbs/bcbs_work.htm

## CHAPTER 2

The Basel I Regulatory Framework and the Cooke Ratio

CAPITAL ADEQUACY

With the aim to protect internationally active banks in the G10 countries against bankruptcy, the Basel Committee developed in 1988 a common solvency ratio, known as the Cooke ratio, named after Peter Cooke, the Chairman of the Basel Committee at this time. According to BCBS (1988), through this new solvency ratio, the fundamental objective is to "*strengthen the soundness and stability of the international banking system* [. . .] *with a view to diminishing competitive inequality among international banks*". Stated differently, credit institutions competing for the same loans should comply with the same capital-backing constraints, and thus set aside roughly the same amount of capital. Although the Cooke ratio focuses on credit risk, the Committee acknowledges that other types of risk, such as interest risk, exchange rate risk, concentration risk and the investment risk on securities, should also be considered in assessing overall capital adequacy.[1]

The Cooke ratio is a solvency ratio because it requires international banks to hold capital for credit equal to at least 8% of the Risk-Weighted Assets (RWA). For example, it means that to lend €100m, a bank should own at least €8m of capital. The Cooke ratio is defined as follows:

$$\text{Cooke ratio} = \frac{\text{Capital}}{\text{RWA}} \geq 8\%$$

where RWA is defined as the bank's asset weighted by its Risk Weight (RW). These asset weights or scores serve to differentiate the capital load according to their quality in terms of credit standing. The risk scale of on-balance-sheet assets starts at 0% for the least risky, up to 100% for the riskiest.[2] The following assets are risk-weighted at 0%:

- Cash
- Gold

- Claims on OECD governments and central banks
- Claims on governments and central banks outside the OECD and denominated in the national currency

The following assets are risk-weighted at 100%:

- Longer-term claims on banks incorporated outside the OECD
- Claims on commercial companies owned by the public sector
- Claims on private-sector commercial enterprises

In between, two categories of on-balance-sheet assets are risk-weighted at 20% and 50%, respectively. The first category includes:

- Claims on all banks with residual maturity < 1 year
- Longer-term claims on OECD incorporated banks
- Claims on public-sector entities within the OECD

Loans secured on residential property are risk-weighted at 50%.

The required capital or capital charge under the Basel I framework through the Cooke ratio is straightforward to calculate. You may do this by simply multiplying the assets in each risk category by the risk weight, and then multiply the result by 8%. Let us consider a commercial loan of value $100. As indicated above, this asset is risk-weighted at 100%. The resulting capital charge for credit risk is thus $100 × 100% × 8% = $8. In this toy example, a risk weight of 100% results in a Cooke ratio of 8%. For a mortgage, backed by real property, the same loan will result in a capital charge of $100 × 50% × 8% = $4, because this asset is risk-weighted at 50%.

To calculate the Cooke ratio, we also need to know the Basel Committee on Banking Supervision (BCBS)'s definition of capital. The Committee places the emphasis on equity capital and disclosed reserves as the key constituents of capital. The rationale is that it is wholly visible in the published accounts and common to all countries' banking systems. The Committee further adds that this component of capital has a significant impact on profit margins and a bank's ability to compete. This explains why it is called Core Capital or Tier 1 Capital.

- **Core Capital (Tier I Capital)**
  - Paid-up capital (issued and fully paid ordinary shares/common stock)
  - Disclosed reserves (general and legal reserves)

The Committee also includes other important and legitimate constituents of a bank's capital base, defining the Supplementary Capital or Tier 2 Capital.

- **Supplementary Capital (Tier 2 Capital)**
  - Undisclosed reserves (other provisions against probable losses)
  - Assets revaluation reserves
  - General provisions/general loan-loss reserves
  - Subordinated term debt (maturity > 5 years)
  - Hybrid debt/equity instruments

The sum of Tier 1 and Tier 2 elements is eligible for inclusion in the capital base.[3] Besides, the following deductions must be made from this capital base in order to calculate the Cooke ratio:

- Investment in unconsolidated banking and financial subsidiary companies and investments in the capital of other banks and financial institutions
- Goodwill

There are two additional constraints for banks:

i. They must hold at least 50% of their capital base in Tier 1 Core Capital. As seen before, Tier 1 Core Capital includes equity capital and published reserves from post-tax earnings. This condition can be expressed as

$$\text{Tier 1 Core Capital} \geq \text{Tier 2 Supplementary Capital}$$

ii. Their ratio of Tier 1 Core Capital to risk-weighted assets must be equal to or higher than 4%. This condition can be expressed as

$$\text{Tier 1 Core Capital/RWA} \geq 4\%$$

WORKED EXAMPLE 1: COMPUTATION OF THE COOKE RATIO

The assets of a bank are composed of $50m of cash, $250m of French OATs (government bonds), $150m of Singapore T-bills, $80m of loans fully secured by mortgage on residential property and $300m of corporate loans tailored to the funding of short-term cash flow issues and growth projects. The bank liabilities structure includes $35m of common stocks and $15m of subordinated debt.[4]

Figure 3 shows a simplified typical bank balance sheet, which reports some items mentioned in the example above.

We also reproduce the capital adequacy ratio: Cooke ratio $= \dfrac{\text{Capital}}{\text{RWA}} \geq 8\%$.

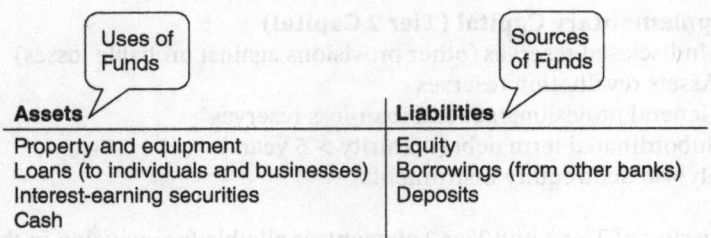

FIGURE 3   A simplified bank balance sheet

The data given in our example are either uses or sources of funds. Obviously, common stocks and subordinated debt are liabilities because they refer to equity and borrowings in **Figure 3**, respectively. Cash is the most liquid asset and can be used to purchase other assets. This explains why cash is registered as a source of funds in the balance sheet. Financial analysts worldwide say "cash is king". Then, we have the French OATs, Singapore T-bills, and residential mortgage and corporate loans. All of these are assets referred to interest-earning securities (OATs and T-bills) and loans (residential mortgage and corporate loans) in **Figure 3**. Some insights about these different assets and liabilities are provided in **Box 1**.

Both assets and liabilities are related to "Capital" in the Cooke ratio (numerator). As seen before, the common stocks are paid-up capital and are thus defined as Tier 1 Core Capital under the Basel I framework. Subordinated term debt is referred to as Tier 2 Supplementary Capital. We thus have the following:

Tier 1 Capital (Core Capital) = $35m of common stocks
+
Tier 2 Capital (Supplementary Capital) = $15m of subordinated debt

= $50m of Capital

The next step is the RWA calculation; that is, the Cooke ratio denominator. For this, each asset is weighted by its corresponding risk weight as defined previously:

- $50m of cash → RW = 0%
- $250m of French OAT → RW = 0%
- $150m of Singapore T-bills → RW = 100%
- $80m of residential mortgage loans → RW = 50%
- $300m of corporate loans → RW = 100%

The French OATs are risk-weighted at 0% because France is an OECD member country. The Singapore T-bills are risk-weighted at 100% because

Singapore is a non-OECD member country. The RWA s are obtained by multiplying each bank's asset value with the corresponding risk weight:

- Cash → RWA = $50m × 0% = 0
- French OAT → RWA = $250m × 0% = 0
- Singapore T-bills → RWA = $150m × 100% = $150m
- Residential mortgage loans → RWA = $80m × 50% = $40m
- Corporate loans → RWA = $300 × 100% = $300m

Total = $490m

The risk-weighted assets of the bank are then equal to $490m. The capital adequacy Cooke ratio is thus

$$\text{Cooke ratio} = \frac{\$50m}{\$490m} = 10.20\%$$

We conclude that this bank complies with the regulatory requirements because its Cooke ratio is higher than 8%, and its Tier 1 Core Capital ratio is also higher than 4%:

$$\text{Tier 1 capital ratio} = \frac{\text{Common equity}}{\text{RWA}} = \frac{\$35m}{\$490m} = 7.14\%$$

Box 1

Examples of banks' assets and liabilities

o **OATs** (Obligations Assimilables du Trésor) are government bonds issued by the French Republic that are backed by the full faith and credit of the State. Retail investors can purchase fixed-rate OATs with maturities ranging from 2 to 50 years. These bonds have annual coupons and are redeemable at maturity. Since 1985, OATs have been the State's preferred source of long-term financing. France is an OECD member country.

o **T-bills** (Treasury bills) are short-term, tradable Singapore Government Securities (SGS) that are issued at a discount to their face value. The Government issues 6-month and 1-year T-bills. They are fully backed by the Singapore Government. Singapore is a non-OECD member country.

o **Corporate lending** is tailored to specific business requirements. Cash-flow lending is unsecured loans that belong to the class of corporate loans. They enable well-established companies with a stable outlook in terms of long-term credit rating to meet immediate cash requirements.

Now, let's assume that the bank in our example makes the decision to change its liabilities structure in this way: $15m of common stocks and $35m of subordinated debt. Its Cooke ratio is still equal to

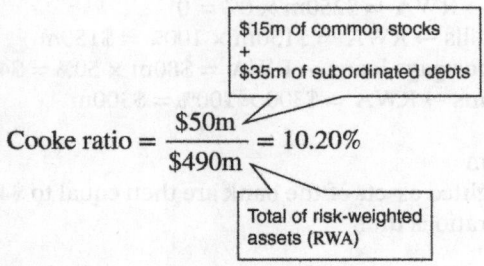

$$\text{Cooke ratio} = \frac{\$50m}{\$490m} = 10.20\%$$

However, its Tier 1 Core Capital ratio is modified as follows:

$$\text{Tier 1 capital ratio} = \frac{\text{Common equity}}{\text{RWA}} = \frac{\$15m}{\$490m} = 3.06\%$$

Therefore, the Tier 1 Core Capital ratio is no longer equal to or higher than 4%, meaning that the condition (ii) Tier 1 Core Capital/RWA ≥ 4% is violated. Moreover, the condition (i) Tier 1 Core Capital ≥ Tier 2 Supplementary Capital is also violated, since the Tier 2 Supplementary Capital ratio is equal to

$$\text{Tier 2 capital ratio} = \frac{\text{Subordinated debt}}{\text{RWA}} = \frac{\$35m}{\$490m} = 7.14\%$$

We know that the Tier 2 capital ratio (7.14%) cannot exceed the Tier 1 capital ratio (3.06%). As a conclusion, our bank is no longer compliant with the Basel I regulatory requirements.

The Basel I accord is the first attempt to define a target standard ratio of capital to weighted risk assets: (Tier 1 + Tier 2 capital)/RWA ≥ 8%. The Cooke ratio is a target ratio because the Basel I accord requires banks to maintain a Cooke ratio of 8%. This accord has been extensively criticized by the banking industry. First, because it does not encompass other types of risk, such as market and operational risks, for example, that may also be impactful. Second, because it adopts a too simplistic and arbitrary method for setting the risk weights. Credit risk weights are not derived from any probability of insolvency thresholds or measures, but are the end result of a long process of negotiation between the Basel Committee, the G10 countries and the supervisory authorities worldwide. The risk weights might be based on the actual risk of each asset instead.

NOTES

1. Capital adequacy for internationally active banks consists of complying with the minimum levels of capital set by the agreed Basel framework under review.
2. There is also a grid for the credit risk off-balance-sheet items. It consists of applying credit conversion factors to the different types of off-balance-sheet instrument or transaction. The interested reader is referred to Annex 3, p. 23 of BCBS (1988).
3. Subject to certain limitations and restrictions, see BCBS (1988), Annex 1, p. 17 for details.
4. We assume maturity > 5 years.

## CHAPTER 3

Amendment to the Basel I Framework to Incorporate Market Risks

THE ADVENT OF MARKET RISK

In January 1996, the Basel Committee issued a document to amend the Capital Accord of July 1988 to take account of market risks. This new risk measurement framework set capital requirements for market risks. As from the end of 1997, banks were required to measure and apply capital charges in respect of their market risks in addition to their credit risks.

According to BCBS (1996), market risk is defined as *"the risk of losses in on and off-balance sheet positions arising from movements in market prices"*. This definition encompasses:

- The risks pertaining to *interest rate-related instruments* and *equities* in the trading book.
- *Foreign exchange risk* and *commodities risk* throughout the bank.

A bank's *trading book* includes financial instruments intended for active trading, such as equities, debt, commodities, foreign exchange and other financial contracts intentionally held for short-term resale to benefit from short-term price fluctuations. It contrasts with the *banking book*, whose financial assets should be held until maturity.

The boundary between the financial instruments to be included in the trading book and the banking book is clearly defined in BCBS (2019a, p. 3). In short, the trading book includes financial instruments subject to market risk capital requirements, whereas those subject to credit risk capital requirements are registered in the banking book. This distinction is important because it has a significant impact on a bank's risk capital requirements. Moving instruments between the trading and banking books for regulatory arbitrage is strictly forbidden. Should a capital benefit result from this switch, the difference in capital will be recorded as a Pillar 1 capital surcharge.[1] It is also worth mentioning that banks are required to manage the market risk in their trading book on a daily basis (i.e., at the close of each trading day). The aim is to ensure that the capital requirements are met on a continuous basis.

The minimum capital requirement is expressed in terms of two calculated charges. The capital charge for specific risk is designed to protect against factors related to the financial instrument itself. Such factors are also known as idiosyncratic. They are opposed to general market risk or factors related to the evolution of financial markets, called systematic factors or risk.

As an example, for interest rate risk, BCBS (1996) indicates that "*the capital requirements for general market risk are designed to capture the risk of loss arising from changes in market interest rates*". In contrast, "*the capital charge for specific risk is designed to protect against an adverse movement in the price of an individual security owing to factors related to the individual issuer*". This holds true for an equity position risk, whether it is a short or a long position. The specific risk refers to holding a long or short position in an individual equity, and the general market risk to the overall net position in an equity market.[2]

The risk measurement framework set by BCBS (1996) offers two broad methodologies to market risk capital requirements: a standardized method and an internal model-based approach.[3] The capital charge under the standardized measurement approach is straightforward. The bank applies a fixed capital charge for each financial instrument related to market risk, and then the resulting capital charges are summed arithmetically. In contrast, the internal model-based approach allows banks to use risk measures derived from their own internal risk models. It should be noted, however, that the use of this alternative is conditional upon the approval of the bank's supervisory authority, based on the fulfilment of seven sets of conditions (BCBS, 1996):

1. *Certain general criteria concerning the adequacy of the risk management system.*
2. *Qualitative standards for internal oversight of the use of models, notably by management.*
3. *Guidelines for specifying an appropriate set of market risk factors (i.e., the market rates and prices that affect the value of banks' positions).*
4. *Quantitative standards setting out the use of common minimum statistical parameters for measuring risk.*
5. *Guidelines for stress testing.*
6. *Validation procedures for external oversight of the use of models.*
7. *Rules for banks which use a mixture of models and the standardized approach.*

Given the scope of this book, which is not dedicated to Basel banking regulations strictly speaking, the point is not to go into the details of each one. Later in the book, we will review the quantitative fourth and fifth sets of conditions above. For now, it is enough to know that banks must use a risk metric called Value-at-Risk (VaR) to compute the market risk capital charge under Basel II. A stress-testing programme is used to identify extreme risk events, that is large losses with a weak probability of occurrence but a huge impact on banks' business continuity. Stress testing is *"a key component of a bank's assessment of its capital position [...] aimed at identifying steps the bank can take to reduce its risk and conserve capital"* (BCBS, 1996, p. 46).

As for their risk management system (first set of conditions), banks must demonstrate that it is *"conceptually sound and implemented with integrity"* (BCBS, 1996, p. 38). At the core of this system is the internal market risk measurement model.

To measure market risks, a bank should be able to specify an appropriate set of market risk factors (i.e., the market rates and prices that affect the value of its trading positions). The 1996 amended accord provides banks with guidelines for specifying these risk factors. Taking the example of equity prices, BCBS (1996, p. 43) indicates: *"at a minimum, there should be a risk factor that is designed to capture market wide movements in equity prices (e.g., a market index)"*. It is also mentioned that it is possible to calculate a "beta-equivalent" position through a market model of equity price returns such as the CAPM (Capital Asset Pricing Model).

Qualitative standards for internal oversight of the use of market risk models (second set of conditions) are an important part of the adequacy of a bank's risk management system. For example, banks are required to have *"an independent risk control unit that is responsible for the design and implementation of their risk management system"*.

COMPUTING THE CAPITAL CHARGE FOR CREDIT AND MARKET RISKS

There is a great difference with the rules of the Cooke ratio (BCBS, 1988), where the credit risk capital charge was calculated using different weights given the credit instrument under review. Now, the bank directly computes the market risk capital requirement using either the standardized method or the internal model-based approach. The Cooke ratio is thus extended in this way:

$$\text{Cooke ratio} = \frac{\text{Capital}}{\text{RWA} + \boxed{12.5} \times \mathbb{C}_{MR}} \geq 8\%$$

The reciprocal of the
minimum capital ratio of 8%

$$8\% = \frac{1}{12.5}$$

where $\mathbb{C}_{MR}$ denotes the market risk capital and Capital is the bank's total capital defined as Tier 1 capital + Tier 2 capital (the same as in the 1988 Basel Accord) + a third tier of capital (Tier 3 capital), consisting of short-term subordinated debt.[4]

What is surprising in the above Cooke ratio is 12.5, the reciprocal of the minimum capital ratio of 8%. Where does it come from and what is it for? The explanation lies in the difference in calculating the capital requirement for credit risk and market risk. In the former case, the capital charge is based on the risk-weighted assets, whereas for market risk, the capital charge is calculated directly on the basis of the measurement systems: the standardized measurement method or the internal model-based approach. This makes a huge difference.

The Basel Committee explains that "*to ensure consistency in the calculation of the capital requirements of credit and market risks, an explicit numerical link will be created by multiplying the measure of market risk by 12.5 (i.e., the reciprocal of the minimum capital ratio of 8%) and adding the resulting figure to the sum of risk-weighted assets compiled for credit risk purposes*" (BCBS, 1996, p. 8). To have a better understanding of this statement, we can rewrite the Cooke ratio defined above as follows:

$$\text{Capital} \geq 8\% \times \left(\text{RWA} + 12.5\mathbb{C}_{MR} \right)$$
$$\text{Capital} \geq 8\% \times \text{RWA} + (8\% \times 12.5\mathbb{C}_{MR})$$
$$\geq 8\% \times \text{RWA} + (\underbrace{8\% \times 12.5}\mathbb{C}_{MR})$$

$= 1$
Since 12.5 is the
reciprocal of 8%

We thus have

$$\text{Capital} \geq \underbrace{8\% \times \text{RWA}}_{\mathbb{C}_{CR}} + \mathbb{C}_{MR}$$

Credit risk capital
requirement

Multiplying the measure of market risk by 12.5 is only useful for creating a numerical link between the calculation of the capital requirement for market and credit risks.[5]

WORKED EXAMPLE 2: COMPUTATION OF THE EXTENDED COOKE RATIO

We still consider the bank of Worked Example 1. For the sake of simplicity, we assume that the market risk on equity portfolio of this bank is $35m (i.e., the amount of common stocks as reported in its liabilities structure). Complying with BCBS (1996), this bank uses an internal model based on 99% VaR to estimate its portfolio loss. Its 99% VaR equals $2.8m.

→ Question: Does this bank meet the minimum capital requirement of 8%?

In order to check whether this bank complies with the capital requirement of 8%, we simply need to compute its Cooke ratio:

> Common stocks (Tier 1 capital) = $35m
> +
> Subordinated debt (Tier 2 capital) = $15m
> = $50m of capital

$$\text{Cooke ratio} = \frac{\underbrace{\$50m}}{\underbrace{\$490m}_{\substack{\text{Risk weighted} \\ \text{assets (RWA)}}} + 12.5 \times \underbrace{\$2.8m}_{\text{99\% Value-at-Risk (VaR)}}} = 9.52\%$$

As a conclusion, using its internal model (99% VaR), the bank complies with the minimum capital requirement of 8% (Cooke ratio > 8%). What happens if the bank uses the standardized measurement method instead?

To answer this, we need to know if the bank's portfolio is well-diversified and liquid. What for? Simply because it will impact the specific market risk charge. Indeed, BCBS (1996, p. 19) indicates the following for a portfolio of stocks: "*The capital charge for specific risk will be 8%, unless the portfolio is both well-diversified and liquid, in which case the charge will be 4%*".

Let's assume the portfolio under review is both diversified and liquid. The corresponding capital charge for specific risk will thus be equal to 4%. Regarding the general market risk charge, it is simpler since marketability (liquidity) and concentration (diversification) are not considered and, as a result, the capital charge for general risk will be 8% (BCBS, 1996, p. 19). At the end of the day, the corresponding risk capital charge for the bank's portfolio will be 4% (specific risk) + 8% (general market risk) = 12%.

When using the standardized method, the market risk capital measurement of the bank, denoted as $\mathbb{C}_{MR}$, is equal to

$$\mathbb{C}_{MR} = 12\% \times \underbrace{\$35m}_{} = \$4.2m$$

4% (specific risk)
+
8% (general market risk)
= 12%

Common stocks
(Tier 1 capital)

Therefore, the Cooke ratio becomes

$$\text{Cooke ratio} = \frac{\$50}{\$490m + 12.5 \times 4.2} = 9.21\%$$

Market risk
capital = $\mathbb{C}_{MR}$

We conclude that the bank still meets the minimum capital requirement of 8%. It should be noted, however, that it does not hold true each and every time. Generally speaking, the internal model-based approach is more "advantageous" for banks than the standardized measurement method. This is due to diversification.[6]

In contrast to the VaR (internal model-based) approach, the standardized method is unable to take diversification into account. The decrease in risk generated through diversification, and measured with the VaR indicator, leads to lower capital requirements, which is obviously appealing for banks. That explains why a vast majority of banks made the decision to implement internal models in the 2000s.

NOTES

1. Pillar 1 corresponds to minimum capital requirements under the Basel II regulatory framework (published in June 2004). It explains how to compute the capital charge for credit risk, market risk and operational risk, as will be explained further.
2. The overall net position is the difference between the sum of the long positions and the sum of the short ones.
3. The four market risks addressed by BCBS (1996) are interest rate, equity position, foreign exchange and commodities risk.
4. Banks are entitled to use Tier 3 capital solely to support market risks. This third tier of capital is limited to 250% of a bank's Tier 1 capital.
5. In the terms of the Basel Committee, the aim is to create "trading book notional risk-weighted assets".
6. Harry Markowitz devised Modern Portfolio Theory in 1952 (see Markowitz, 1952) and won the 1990 Nobel Prize in Economics. Since then, we know that diversifying assets in a portfolio decreases its risk.

## CHAPTER 4

Implementation of the Basel II Framework

THE THREE PILLARS

The finalized Basel II framework was published in June 2004, but its effective implementation date was June 2006, due to the difficulty the regulator and the banking industry experienced in reaching a general agreement, more or less acceptable for both. As illustrated in **Figure 4**, the Basel II framework is designed along three main strands:

- The first pillar (Minimum Capital Requirements) explains how to calculate the total minimum capital requirements for credit risk, market risk and operational risk. For the most part, the definition of eligible regulatory capital (constituents of capital in **Figure 4**), as outlined in the 1988 Accord and extended in BCBS (1996), remains in place.[1]
- The second pillar (Supervisory Review Process) is intended to ensure that banks have adequate capital to support all the risks in their business; it discusses the key principles of the internal assessment process with respect to banking risks.
- The third pillar (Market Discipline) develops a set of disclosure requirements to encourage safe and sound banking practices.

In what follows, we focus on the first pillar because minimum regulatory capital requirements play the most important role in Basel II. First of all, they ensure that banks maintain adequate capital. Moreover, since they are supposed to accurately reflect a bank's risk, minimum regulatory capital requirements provide more effective triggers for prompt corrective action.

The new solvency ratio was named the McDonough ratio after William McDonough, the Chairman of the Basel Committee on Banking Supervision (1998–2003). It introduces a third capital charge for operational risk in

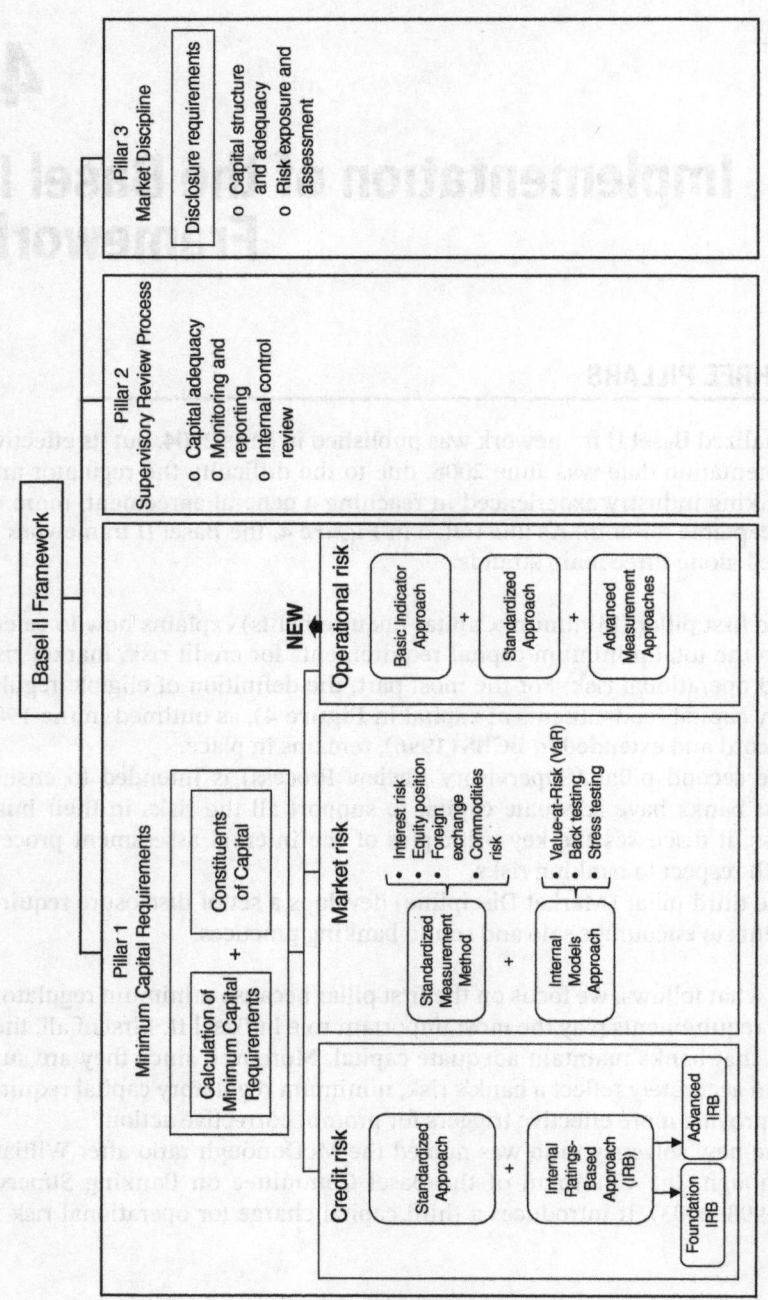

FIGURE 4 The three pillars of the Basel II framework

addition to credit and market risks. Regarding the first pillar, the minimum capital requirement is calculated through the McDonough ratio as follows:

$$\text{McDonough ratio} = \frac{\text{Capital}}{\text{RWA} + 12.5 \times \mathbb{C}_{MR} + 12.5 \times \mathbb{C}_{OR}} \geq 8\%$$

The capital charge for
operational risk

With the McDonough ratio, the required capital for credit risk is still calculated through the Risk-Weighted Assets (RWA), as it was under BCBS (1996), but using strongly modified methods.

Banks may choose between two broad methodologies for calculating their capital requirements for credit risk. One alternative is the standardized approach where credit risk is measured in a standardized manner, supported by external credit assessments. The Basel Committee follows the Standard & Poor's credit rating as a benchmark, but any other External Credit Assessment Institution (ECAI) can be eligible. However, ECAIs must meet the following six criteria set by the national supervisors: objectivity, independence, international access/transparency, disclosure, resources and credibility. BCBS (2006, pp. 27–28) provides a detailed definition of each one. Under this approach, the capital charge is computed through a mapping process consisting of assigning the standardized risk weights to the credit rating.

The other alternative is the internal ratings-based approach, where banks are allowed to use their internal rating systems for credit risk but are subject to the explicit approval of the supervisor.

In contrast, there have been no great changes in the calculation of the capital charge for market risk. The key points of the BCBS (1996) framework mentioned previously hold true.[2] The capital charge for market risk is still calculated directly (i.e., without using RWA) and the capital charge for operational risk as well. Let's illustrate the calculation of the McDonough ratio with a toy example.

WORKED EXAMPLE 3: COMPUTATION OF THE MCDONOUGH SOLVENCY RATIO

We consider a bank with the following information: risk-weighted assets for credit risk (RWA) of $350m, capital charge for market risk $\left(\mathbb{C}_{MR}\right)$ of $20m and capital charge for operational risk $\left(\mathbb{C}_{OR}\right)$ of $7m.

To compute the required capital charge ($\mathbb{C}$) for this bank, we can start by rewriting the McDonough ratio as follows, for the sake of convenience:

$$\mathbb{C} = 8\% \times \left(RWA + 12.5 \times \mathbb{C}_{MR} + 12.5 \times \mathbb{C}_{OR} \right)$$

$$\mathbb{C} = 8\% \times (RWA + 12.5 \times \mathbb{C}_{MR} + 8\% \times 12.5 \times \mathbb{C}_{OR})$$

$$= 8\% \times RWA + \underbrace{8\% \times 12.5}_{} \times \mathbb{C}_{MR} + \underbrace{8\% \times 12.5}_{} \times \mathbb{C}_{OR}$$

12.5 is the reciprocal of the minimum capital ratio of 8%
(8% × 12.5 = 1)

We thus have

$$\mathbb{C} = 8\% \times RWA + \mathbb{C}_{MR} + \mathbb{C}_{OR}$$

$$\mathbb{C} = 8\% \times \$350m + \$20m + \$7m$$

$$= \underbrace{8\% \times \$350m + \$20m}_{} + \$7m$$

Capital charge for
credit risk = $28m

$$\mathbb{C} = \$55m$$

The capital requirement for this bank is \$55m. Credit risk represents 50.9% of total risk.[3]

THE INTERNAL RATINGS-BASED APPROACH TO CREDIT RISK

The mechanics of the Internal Ratings-Based (IRB) approach to credit risk are based on four main risk components:

- **Probability of Default (PD).** PD measures the default risk of the debtor. Its time horizon is set to 1 year. According to BCBS (2006, p. 100), a default is considered to have occurred with regard to a particular obligor when either or both of the two following events have taken place: (i) *the bank considers that the obligor is unlikely to pay its credit obligations to the bank in full* and (ii) *the obligor is past due more than 90 days on any material credit obligation to the bank.*
- **Exposure at Default (EAD).** EAD is defined as the outstanding debt at the time of default. This is the loss exposure for a bank when a debtor defaults on a loan, that is the principal amount of the loan.
- **Loss Given Default (LGD).** LGD is the proportion of a credit that is lost in the event of default. LGD is expressed as an expected percentage of EAD. It is common practice to define LGD from the recovery rate $\mathcal{R}$ (generally defined as a fixed ratio of the outstanding debt), such as

LGD $\cong 1 - \mathcal{R}$. Then, the Expected Loss (EL) due to the default can be estimated as the product of these two risk components: EAD (expressed in monetary units) and LGD (measured as a percentage). For example, if EAD equals \$15m and LGD is set to 75%, then the EL due to default is \$15m × 75% = \$11.25m.

- **Effective Maturity (M).** This measures the default risk of the debtor until the duration of the credit (to be calculated when the duration of the credit is not equal to 1 year).

Under the IRB method, the Basel Committee makes available two broad approaches: foundation and advanced. In the foundation IRB, banks only compute the PD and rely on supervisory estimates for the other risk components (EAD, LGD and M). In the advanced IRB, banks may estimate all the risk components using their own internal models.[4] The key risk component of both the foundation and advanced IRB is the probability of default, since its estimate is derived from the internal credit model of the bank.

Another requirement to comply with under the IRB approach is for banks to categorize banking-book exposures into broad classes of assets: (i) corporate; (ii) sovereign; (iii) bank; and (iv) equity.[5] For example, BCBS (2006) defines a corporate exposure as a debt obligation of a corporation, partnership or proprietorship. This classification of exposures is derived from the underlying risk characteristics of each asset class and is broadly consistent with established bank practice.

Regarding operational risk, the new risk included in the Basel II framework (see **Figure 4**) is defined as "*the risk of loss resulting from inadequate or failed internal processes, people and systems or from external events*" (BCBS, 2006, p. 144). Legal risk is considered as an operational risk, while strategic and reputational risks are excluded from the above definition.

The Basel II framework offers three methods for calculating operational risk capital charges with an increasing level of sophistication:

- The Basic Indicator Approach.
- The Standardized Approach.
- The Advanced Measurement Approach (AMA).

There are no specific criteria for use of the Basic Indicator Approach, which is the simplest method available. The capital for operational risk is a fixed percentage of annual gross income.

In the Standardized Approach, a bank's activities are divided into eight business lines.[6] For each business line, the capital charge is calculated as a fixed percentage (denoted beta or β and set by the Basel Committee) of its gross income. For example, in corporate finance, the indicator is the gross income generated in the corporate finance business line, not in the whole institution. The beta factor serves as a proxy for the riskiness of the business

TABLE 1 Business lines and beta factors

Business Lines	Beta Factors
Corporate finance (β_1)	18%
Trading and sales (β_2)	18%
Retail banking (β_3)	12%
Commercial banking (β_4)	15%
Payment and settlement (β_5)	18%
Agency services (β_6)	15%
Asset management (β_7)	12%
Retail brokerage (β_8)	12%

Source: Adapted from BCBS (2006), p. 147

line. The total capital charge is the simple summation of the capital charges across each of the business lines. We reproduce in **Table 1** the business lines and the corresponding beta factor.

Under the Advanced Measurement Approach (AMA), the regulatory minimum capital charge is computed from the bank's internal operational risk statistical model. The use of the AMA is subject to supervisory approval. Whatever statistical model is used, *"a bank must demonstrate its operational risk measure meets a soundness standard comparable to that of the internal ratings-based approach for credit risk"* (BCBS, 2006, p. 151).

Since the 2008 financial turmoil, both the number and magnitude of operational risk losses have augmented drastically. It should be acknowledged that the banking industry is fertile ground for the occurrence of operational risk events. **Figure 5** provides the big picture of operational loss types. This is the loss event type classification adopted by the Basel Committee. It should be noted, however, that operational risk losses are not only due to the banking sector. The diesel emission scandal of Volkswagen is a good example.

The definition of each event-type category (Level 1) from BCBS (2023), numbered from 1 to 7 in **Figure 5**, helps us to better understand the concept of operational risk:[7]

① Internal fraud: *"losses due to acts of a type intended to defraud, misappropriate property or circumvent regulations, the law or company policy, excluding diversity/discrimination events, which involves at least one internal party"*.

② External fraud: *"losses due to acts of a type intended to defraud, misappropriate property or circumvent the law, by a third party"*.

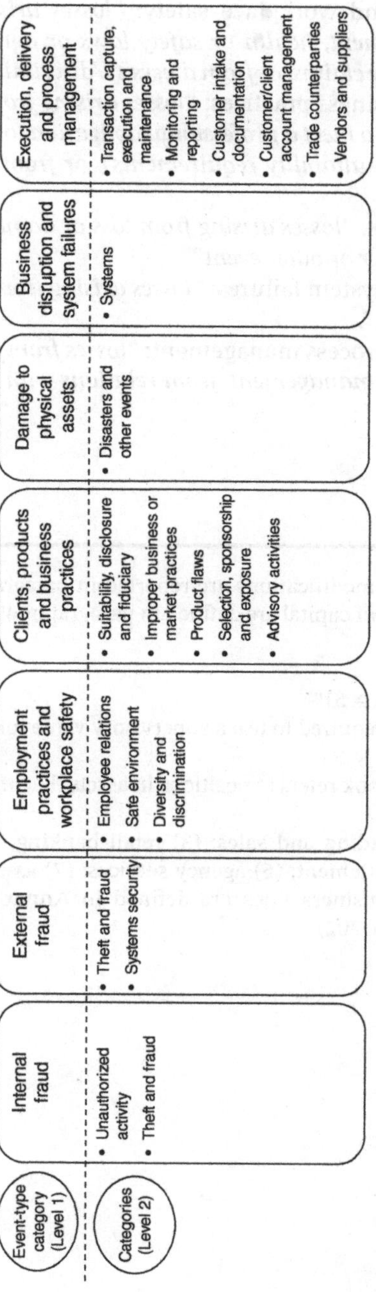

FIGURE 5 Loss event type classification

The figure (rotated) shows a loss event type classification chart with two levels:

Event-type category (Level 1) and **Categories (Level 2)**

① Internal fraud
- Unauthorized activity
- Theft and fraud

② External fraud
- Theft and fraud
- Systems security

③ Employment practices and workplace safety
- Employee relations
- Safe environment
- Diversity and discrimination

④ Clients, products and business practices
- Suitability, disclosure and fiduciary
- Improper business or market practices
- Product flaws
- Selection, sponsorship and exposure
- Advisory activities

⑤ Damage to physical assets
- Disasters and other events

⑥ Business disruption and system failures
- Systems

⑦ Execution, delivery and process management
- Transaction capture, execution and maintenance
- Monitoring and reporting
- Customer intake and documentation
- Customer/client account management
- Trade counterparties
- Vendors and suppliers

③ Employment practices and workplace safety: *"losses arising from acts inconsistent with employment, health or safety laws or agreements, from payment of personal injury claims, or from diversity/discrimination events"*.

④ Clients, products and business practices: *"losses arising from an unintentional or negligent failure to meet a professional obligation to specific clients (including fiduciary and suitability requirements), or from the nature or design of a product"*.

⑤ Damage to physical assets: *"losses arising from loss or damage to physical assets from natural disaster or other event"*.

⑥ Business disruption and system failures: *"losses arising from disruption of business or system failures"*.

⑦ Execution, delivery and process management: *"losses from failed transaction processing or process management, from relations with trade counterparties and vendors"*.

NOTES

1. For the interested reader, the modifications are reported in paragraph 43 of BCBS (2006, p. 12). The constituents of capital are defined in paragraphs 49 (i) to 49 (xviii), pages 14 to 18.
2. See Chapter 3.
3. We have: $28m/$55m = 50.9\% \cong 51\%$.
4. In some cases, banks may be required to use a supervisory value for one or more of the risk components.
5. Remember that the banking book refers to positions in assets that are expected to be held until maturity.
6. (1) Corporate finance; (2) trading and sales; (3) retail banking; (4) commercial banking; (5) payment and settlement; (6) agency services; (7) asset management; (8) retail brokerage. These business lines are defined in Annex 8: Mapping of Business Lines (BCBS, 2006, p. 302).
7. See BCBS (2023).

## CHAPTER 5

A Guided Tour of the Basel III Framework

THE RATIONALE FOR A NEW REGULATORY FRAMEWORK

The BCBS (2010) document is the Basel Committee's reform package to address the market failures revealed by the financial crisis. The aim is to *"improve risk management and governance as well as strengthen banks' transparency and disclosures"* (BCBS, 2010, p. 1).

At the peak of the financial crisis, the markets lost confidence in the solvency and liquidity of the banking sector as a whole. As a result, many banking institutions weakened and, due to spillover effects, this weakness in the banking system was quickly transmitted to the global economy. It should be noted, however, that a regulatory reform such as Basel III, focused on higher capital and liquidity requirements, affects banks' lending rates and, in so doing, affects the path of economic activity. This spillover effect or transmission belt is illustrated in **Figure 6**.

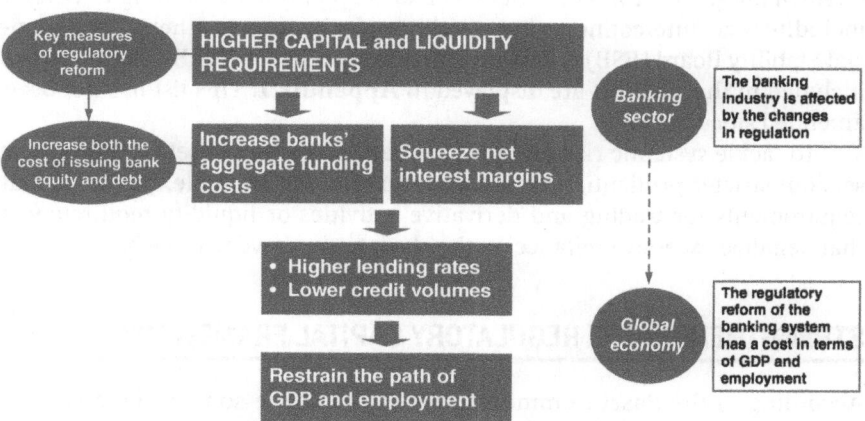

FIGURE 6 Tracing the real economy implications of tighter financial conditions

The Basel III international regulatory framework initiates both micro- and macro-prudential regulation measures. Both approaches share the same goal of strengthening the banking system's resilience. The micro-prudential measures aim to increase the bank-level resilience to periods of stress. They deal with individual banking institutions. In contrast, the macro-prudential approach copes with system-wide risks as well as the procyclical amplification of these risks over time.

Procyclicality amplifies financial shocks throughout the banking system, financial markets and the global economy over the time dimension. The concept of procyclicality has been luminously defined by Jean-Pierre Landau, Deputy Governor of the Bank of France, as follows: "*Strictly speaking, procyclicality refers to the tendency of financial variables to fluctuate around a trend during the economic cycle. Increased procyclicality thus simply means fluctuations with broader amplitude*".[1] It is well known that banks are procyclical and thus will experience more and more defaults as the global economy gets worse. Such procyclicality dynamics were one of the most destabilizing factors of the 2008 crisis.

Of course, both micro- and macro-prudential approaches are interrelated since a greater resilience at the bank level (micro) decreases the risk of system-wide shocks (macro). This points to a key element of the Basel III regulatory framework: systemic risk and interconnectedness. Like procyclicality dynamics, excessive interconnectedness among the so-called Global Systemically Important Banks (G-SIBs) is also a transmitter of shocks to the financial system and broader economy.

A G-SIB is a bank whose "*systemic risk profile is deemed to be of such importance that the bank's failure would trigger a wider financial crisis and threaten the global economy*".[2] Such banks are identified according to criteria including size, interconnectedness and complexity, among others. The Financial Stability Board (FSB) publishes and updates a list of G-SIBs. The 30 banks included in the 2022 list are displayed in **Appendix 1**. This list has not been amended since 2019.

To tackle systemic risk and interconnectedness, the Basel III framework sets out stricter prudential regulation measures. For example, higher capital requirements for trading and derivative activities or liquidity requirements that penalize excessive reliance on the short term, as we will see below.

STRENGTHENING THE REGULATORY CAPITAL FRAMEWORK

According to the Basel Committee, one of the key lessons of the crisis has been the need to raise the resilience of the global banking system by strengthening the Basel II regulatory capital framework. The lack of high-quality capital in the banking sector was a key destabilizing factor during the crisis. To overcome problems of quantity and quality of the regulatory capital base, the Committee implemented a set of major reforms to raise the quality, consistency and transparency of the capital base. These reforms aim at backing banks' risk exposures with a high-quality capital base. To this end, they increase capital requirements for the trading book and put common equity, *"the highest quality component of a bank's capital"* (BCBS, 2010, p. 12), at the core of the new definition of capital.

As shown in **Figure 7**, total regulatory capital is the sum of the following components: Tier 1 Capital (going-concern capital), including Common Equity Tier 1 (CET1) and Additional Tier 1 (AT1), and Tier 2 Capital (gone-concern capital). Interestingly, Basel III introduces an explicit going- and gone-concern framework by distinguishing the roles of Tier 1 Capital and Tier 2 Capital.[3] For each of the three categories listed below, there is a set of criteria that instruments are required to meet before inclusion in the relevant category. All these elements are subject to limits and minima:

- Common Equity Tier 1 must be at least 4.5% of Risk-Weighted Assets (RWA) at all times.
- Tier 1 Capital must be at least 6.0% of RWA at all times.
- Total Capital (Tier 1 Capital + Tier 2 Capital) must be at least 8.0% of RWA at all times.

Regulatory capital under Basel III focuses on high-quality capital. To this end, the predominant form of Tier 1 Capital is common shares and retained earnings that can absorb losses immediately when they occur (going-concern capital). BCBS (2010) indicates that the remainder of the Tier 1 Capital base is comprised of instruments that are *"subordinated, have fully discretionary non-cumulative dividends or coupons and have neither a maturity date nor an incentive to redeem"*.

Additional Tier 1 capital consists predominantly of instruments issued by the bank that meet the criteria for inclusion in Additional Tier 1 capital and are not included in Common Equity Tier 1 (CET1 in **Figure 7**). For example, to be included in Additional Tier 1 capital, an instrument issued by the bank must be (i) issued and paid-in and (ii) subordinated to depositors, general creditors and subordinated debt of the bank.[4]

Based on the objective to provide loss absorption on a gone-concern basis, Tier 2 Capital (gone-concern capital in **Figure 7**) consists predominantly of instruments issued by the bank that meet the criteria for inclusion in Tier 2 Capital and are not included in Tier 1 Capital. As for Tier 1 Capital, these instruments must also be (i) issued and paid-in and (ii) subordinated to depositors, general creditors and subordinated debt of the bank. However, the

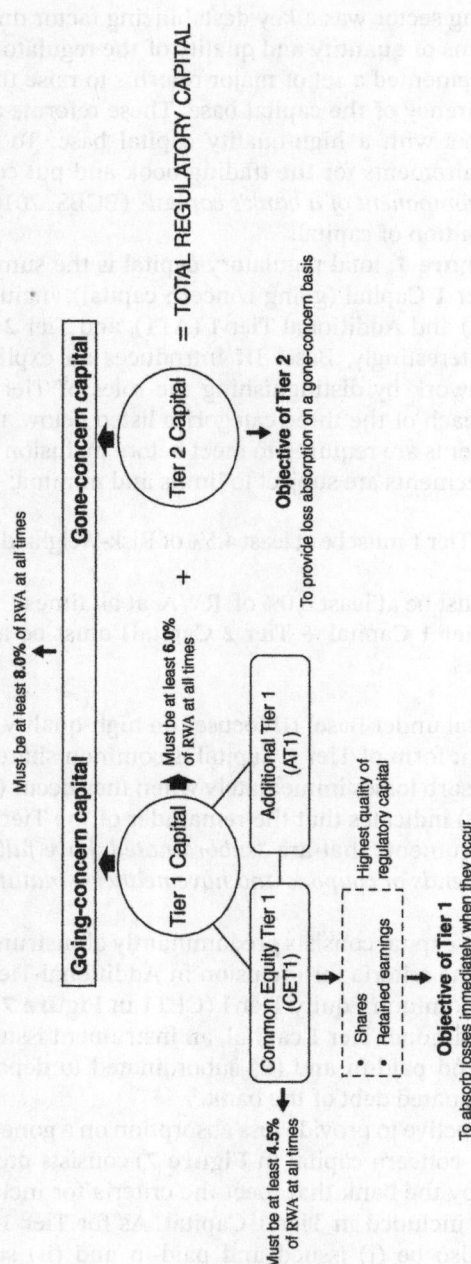

FIGURE 7 Regulatory capital under Basel III

criterion of no maturity date is relaxed as the minimum original maturity of instruments issued by the bank must be at least 5 years. It is also worth mentioning that the investor must have no rights to accelerate the repayment of future scheduled payments (coupon or principal), except in bankruptcy and liquidation.[5]

A NEW GLOBAL LIQUIDITY STANDARD

Basel III introduces international liquidity standards to penalize excessive trust and dependence on the short term. The Committee argues that *"during the early 'liquidity phase' of the financial crisis, many banks—despite adequate levels—still experienced difficulties because they did not manage their liquidity in a prudent manner"* (BCBS, 2010, p. 8).

With the advent of illiquidity, the banking system came under severe pressure and the importance of liquidity to the good functioning of markets came back as a reminder. Following the bankruptcy of Lehman Brothers, the market conditions became tougher due to a loss of confidence in the liquidity of banks. Such a situation required central bank action to support the functioning of money markets.

The global liquidity standards have been developed to prevent bank institutions from a lack of liquidity, which is one of the main sources of systemic risk. To this end, the Basel Committee developed two liquidity ratios. The first one, called the Liquidity Coverage Ratio (LCR), tackles the short-term resilience of a bank's risk profile. It is intended to ensure that the bank has enough available high-quality liquid assets to offset the net cash outflows it could experience under a severe short-term scenario lasting for 1 month.[6]

The second one, called the Net Stable Funding Ratio (NSFR), promotes resilience over a 1-year time horizon. The NSFR requires a minimum amount of stable sources of funding at a bank relative to the liquidity profile of its assets. As such, it is intended to constrain the bank to fund its activities with more stable sources of funding. It is mentioned in BCBS (2010) that the NSFR should help to provide *"a sustainable maturity of the bank's assets and liabilities on an on-going structural basis"*.

The LCR and the NSFR are defined as follows:

$$LCR = \frac{HQLA}{\text{Total net cash outflows}} \geq 100\%$$

where

- HQLA denotes the stock of high-quality liquid assets.
- The denominator is the total net cash outflows over the next 30 days.

The NSFR is simply the amount of Available Stable Funding (ASF) relative to the amount of Required Stable Funding (RSF).

$$\text{NSFR} = \frac{\text{Available stable funding}}{\text{Required stable funding}} \geq 100\%$$

As for the LCR, the NSFR should be equal to 100% on an on-going basis. The amount of ASF corresponds to the total regulatory capital, excluding Tier 2 instruments with residual maturity of less than 1 year, plus the other liabilities to which a 0–100% ASF factor is applied.[7] The amount of RSF is measured based on the broad characteristics of the liquidity risk profile of an institution's assets and Off-Balance-Sheet (OBS) exposures.[8] It is thus the sum of two components: RWA and OBS exposures.

SUPPLEMENTING THE RISK-BASED CAPITAL REQUIREMENT WITH A LEVERAGE RATIO

The Basel III reform also introduces a leverage ratio requirement that is intended to constrain leverage in the banking sector. This leverage ratio acts as a backstop to the risk-based capital measure. According to the Basel Committee, failure to capture major on and off-balance-sheet risks was a key destabilizing factor during the crisis. The Committee further explains (BCBS, 2010, p. 60): "*During the most severe part of the crisis, the banking sector was forced by the market to reduce its leverage in a manner that amplified downward pressure on asset prices, further exacerbating the positive feedback loop between losses, declines in bank capital, and contraction in credit availability*". Such a credit shock may drastically damage the real economy through the spillover effect described in **Figure 8**.

The leverage ratio is designed to act as a credible supplementary measure to the risk-based capital requirements. As such, it enhances the risk coverage of the capital framework. The minimum requirement for the leverage ratio is 3%, as defined below:

$$\text{Leverage ratio} = \frac{\text{Tier 1 capital}}{\text{Total exposures}} \geq 3\%$$

where the total exposure is the sum of (a) on-balance-sheet exposures, (b) derivatives exposures, (c) securities financing transactions,[9] and (d) some adjustments concerning off-balance-sheet items.

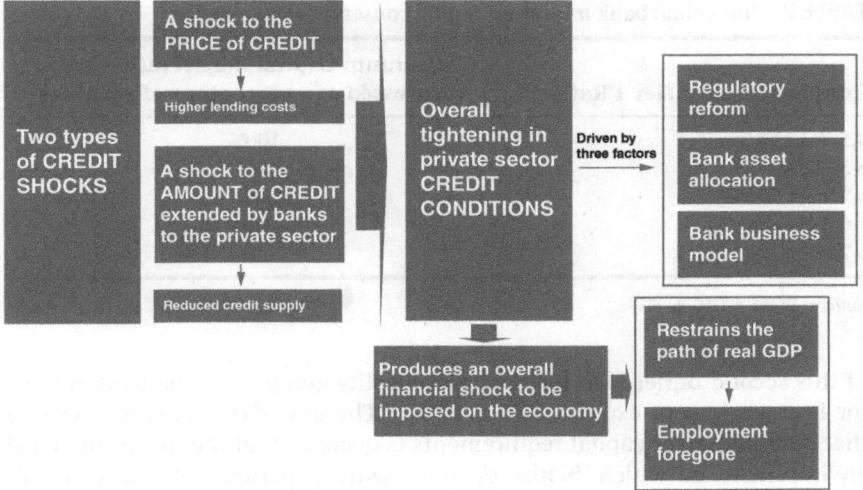

FIGURE 8   Contagion effect of a credit shock to the real economy

CAPITAL BUFFERS

Along with a new definition of risk-based capital, the Basel III regulatory framework also introduces a capital conservation buffer. This buffer is *"designed to ensure that banks build up capital buffers outside the period of stress which can be drawn down as losses are incurred"* (BCBS, 2010, p. 54).

This capital conservation buffer, which is equal to 2.5% of Common Equity Tier 1 (CET1), is established above the regulatory minimum capital requirement. As such, it can be considered as a surplus of CET1, meaning that CET1 must first be used to meet the capital requirements before the remainder can contribute to the capital conservation buffer. This capital conservation rule is established to avoid breaches of minimum capital requirements. The minimum capital conservation standards a bank must meet at various levels of the CET1 capital ratios are reported in **Table 2**.

As an example, to illustrate how **Table 2** works, a bank with a CET1 capital ratio in the range of 5.125–5.75% is required to hold 80% of its earnings in the subsequent financial year. This implies that the total payout cannot be higher than 100% − 80% = 20% in terms of dividends, share buybacks and discretionary bonus payments.

In addition to the conservation capital buffer, BCBS (2010) defines a second capital buffer called the countercyclical capital buffer. The key objective

TABLE 2   Individual bank minimum capital conservation standards

Common Equity Tier 1 Ratio	Minimum Capital Conservation Ratio (expressed as a percentage of earnings)
4.5–5.125%	100%
>5.125–5.75%	80%
>5.75–6.375%	60%
>6.375–7.0%	40%
>7.0%	0%

Source: BCBS (2010, p. 56)

of this second buffer is to reduce procyclicality and protect the banking sector from periods of excess credit growth.[10] The underlying idea is to ensure that banking sector capital requirements take account of the macro-financial environment in which banks operate. During periods of excess credit growth, national authorities may subject banks to a specific countercyclical buffer that varies between 0 and 2.5% to total RWA. Since the countercyclical buffer requirements extend the size of the capital conservation buffer, this measure can increase the CET1 ratio up to 9.5%:

- Common Equity Tier 1 (CET1)   4.5%
- Capital Conservation Buffer (CB)   2.5%
- CET1 + CB   7.0%
- Countercyclical Capital Buffer (CCB)   0–2.5%

→ CET1 + CB + Max. CCB = 7.0% + 2.5% = 9.5%

Lastly, BCBS (2010) mentions capital conservation best practices. For example, when capital buffers have been depleted, a bank is not allowed to *"use predictions of recovery as justification for maintaining generous distributions to shareholders, other capital providers and employees [. . .]* nor to *try and use the distribution of capital as a way to signal their financial strength"* (BCBS, 2010, p. 55). To rebuild buffers, it is recommended that banks reduce discretionary distributions of earnings, such as dividend and staff bonus payments or share buybacks. Another option is to raise new capital from the private sector.

COPING WITH TAIL RISK

In January 2019, the Basel Committee released the final version of the Basel III framework for computing market risk. The objective of the project was to *"develop a new, more robust framework to establish minimum capital requirements for market risk, drawing on the experience of what went wrong in the build-up to the crisis*" (BCBS, 2019b, p. 1).

The January 2019 revision is a response to the shortcomings of the Basel 2.5 reforms (published in July 2009), which did not address key structural weaknesses in the market risk framework:

- *Instruments that should be excluded from, or included in, the trading book.*
  It is unclear to which regulatory book—trading or banking book—instruments are to be assigned. As a result, there is an opportunity for banks to engage in regulatory arbitrage between the capital requirements of the trading book and the banking book. Such an arbitrage is appealing for banking institutions because lower capital requirements apply in one or the other regulatory books. It is less interesting for banking supervision, which is mainly focused on systemic risk.
- *The internal model risk measure—Value-at-Risk (VaR)—used as the basis of market risk capital requirements for trading activities.*
  The Basel 2.5 framework improved significantly the VaR metric (used in the pre-crisis Basel II framework) to take better account of the tail risk—losses that banks can experience in stressed financial markets. This led to the adoption of the so-called stressed VaR—an additional VaR-based risk metric calibrated to address adequate capital requirements in a stressed period.
- *Incentives for banks to take on tail risk.*
  This is probably the most salient drawback of the Basel 2.5 framework. As mentioned before, the stressed VaR was a significant improvement of the VaR risk metric. However, in essence, both VaR and stressed VaR are unable to account for losses that had less than 1% probability of occurring. According to BCBS (2019b, p. 3), a perverse effect of using VaR and its stressed version is *"to hold positions that features significant tail risks but were subject to limited risk in 'normal' conditions"*. In other words, the Basel 2.5 internal model approach is used even where it estimates risk inappropriately. This is a serious concern, since the aim of banking supervision is precisely to reduce such tail risk events—losses with a low probability of occurrence (1%) but with high magnitude and high impact.

To illustrate the danger of heavy reliance on VaR for measuring capital requirements, **Figure 9** plots the new Expected Shortfall (ES) single metric that replaces VaR and stressed VaR in the Basel III framework. The ES is calibrated to better capture tail risk (and to incorporate the risk of market illiquidity, as explained further) that is not accounted for in the existing VaR measure (be it stressed or not). The ES is thus intended to alleviate one of the main deficiencies in the significant market stress.

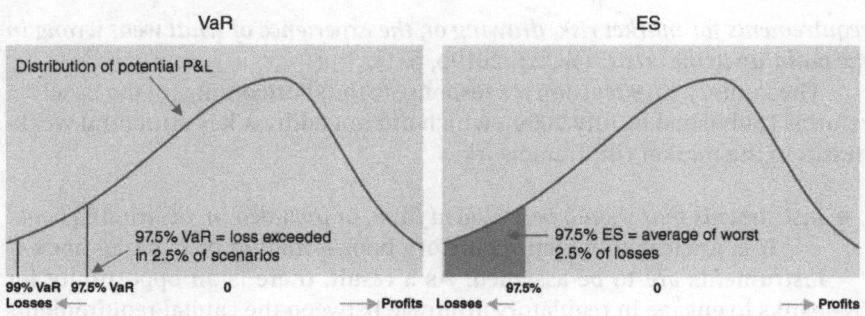

FIGURE 9   Expected Shortfall (ES) compared to Value-at-Risk (VaR)
Source: Adapted from BCBS (2019b, p. 7)

The main point about VaR and ES is never to forget that both are no more than a potential loss estimated over a given time horizon (generally speaking, the next 10 days) for a given confidence level (e.g., 97.5% or 99% as indicated in **Figure 9**). We are therefore talking about estimated and not exact values. It means that the actual loss can be much higher than the potential loss estimated through VaR or ES.

As shown in **Figure 9**, VaR calculates the maximum potential loss at a single cut-off point in the distribution of Profit and Loss (P&L).[11] For example, the 97.5% and 99% cut-off points in **Figure 9** (*x*-axis) mean that the loss is expected to be exceeded only 2.5% and 1% of the time, respectively. The underlying logic of ES is different, since it is interested in the average of any loss that exceeds a given cut-off point in the P&L distribution (*x*-axis). For example, a 99% ES calculates the average of the worst 1% of losses. Similarly, a 97.5% ES will calculate the average of the worst 2.5% of losses. In these two examples, we have two confidence levels α equal to 97.5% and 99%. We thus have $1 - \alpha$ = 2.5% and 1%, respectively.[12]

When the same cut-off point (also known as a percentile) is used to compute both VaR and ES, the value of ES will be higher than the value of VaR, since ES corresponds to the expected loss beyond VaR. This explains why ES is said to be a more conservative risk measure than VaR. In the case of fat-tailed P&L distributions, the difference between ES and VaR values inflates.[13] The 97.5% ES under Basel III and the 99% VaR used in Basel 2.5 produce roughly equivalent outcomes.

A material improvement offered by the ES measure is to tackle the risk of market illiquidity through the definition of different liquidity horizons for different risk factors. BCBS (2019b, p. 7) defines the liquidity horizon as *"the time required to exit or to hedge a risk factor without materially affecting market prices under stressed market conditions"*. The different liquidity classes and horizons are reported in **Table 3**. To integrate the risk of market

TABLE 3 Liquidity horizon (in days) under Basel III

Liquidity Class	Liquidity Horizon
1	10
2	20
3	40
4	60

illiquidity into its calculation, the ES indicator computes the loss that a bank might experience over the liquidity horizon specified in **Table 3** in a period of market stress. This way of calculating ES is of great interest for the banking regulator because it generates higher capital requirements for less liquid factors (i.e., market variables such as interest rates or equity prices that affect the value of financial instruments).

NOTES

1. Jean-Pierre Landau: *Procyclicality – what it means and what could be done.* Remarks by Mr. Jean-Pierre Landau, Deputy Governor of the Bank of France, at the Bank of Spain's Conference on Procyclicality and the Role of Financial Regulation, BIS Review 94/2009, Madrid, 4 May 2009.
2. Source: https://www.risk.net
3. The so-called Tier 3 Capital instruments, which were intended to cover market risks, are cancelled.
4. The comprehensive list of criteria for inclusion in Additional Tier 1 capital is reported in BCBS (2010, pp. 15–16).
5. The comprehensive list of criteria for inclusion in Tier 2 Capital is reported in BCBS (2010, pp. 18–19).
6. The specified scenario is built upon conditions experienced during the 2008 global financial crisis. This is not a worst-case scenario, but it entails significant stress in terms of institution-specific and systemic shocks.
7. The ASF factors to be applied in calculating an institution's total amount of available stable funding are displayed in Table 1 of BCBS (2014a, p. 6).
8. Off-balance-sheet items may expose banking institutions to credit risk, liquidity risk or counterparty risk, which is not reflected on the balance sheet. These include contingent assets or liabilities such as unused commitments, letters of credit and derivatives. A more detailed list of off-balance-sheet items is available in BCBS (2010).
9. BCBS (2014b) defines securities financing transactions as transactions such as repurchase agreements, reverse repurchase agreements, security lending and borrowing and margin lending transactions, where the value of the transactions depends on market valuations and the transactions are often subject to margin agreements.

10. The Basel Committee explains in BCBS (2010, p. 57) that: "*Losses incurred in the banking sector can be extremely large when a downturn is preceded by a period of excess credit growth. These losses can destabilise the banking sector and spark a vicious circle, whereby problems in the financial system can contribute to a downturn in the real economy that then feeds back on to the banking sector*".

11. P&L is produced by banking institutions' risk measurement models.

12. The sum of α and 1 − α will always be equal to one since it is the maximum value for a probability.

13. Fat tails are very common in distributions of financial asset returns. A fat-tail event is often referred to as a black swan, named after the book authored by Taleb (2007). Black swan or tail risk is when something occurs that was unexpected or considered inconceivable (or nearly impossible).

## CHAPTER 6

Climate-Related Financial Risks

In November 2021, the Basel Committee on Banking Supervision (BCBS) published a consultative document in the form of BCBS guidelines titled *Principles for the effective management and supervision of climate-related financial risks*. This document was issued for comments by 16 February 2022. The Committee expected comments from all stakeholders on the proposed principles and requested feedback on three questions. Of the three, the third one is the most comprehensive because it reflects the big picture of climate-related financial risk management: *"How could the transmission of environmental risks to banks' risk profiles be taken into account when considering the potential application of these principles to broader environmental risks in the future? Which key aspects should be considered?"* (BCBS, 2021, p. 10).

Through the publication of this consultative document, the Committee aims to provide banks with guidance on effective management of climate-related financial risks. Interestingly, this document also includes guidance for prudential supervisors. This is the first initiative from the Basel Committee to tackle the challenges—both present and future—arising from climate change.

As observed by the Basel Committee, there is no question that *"banks are potentially exposed to climate-related financial risks regardless of their size, complexity or business model"* (BCBS, 2021, p. 2). Moreover, the potential impacts of climate-related risk drivers could affect the resilience of individual banking institutions and destabilize the banking system. This enhances the need for improved risk management and supervisory practices related to climate-related financial risk.

The consultative document comes in a principles-based format, including a set of 18 high-level principles subdivided into two main categories (see **Figure 10**):

- Guidance on effective management of climate-related financial risks (Principles 1 to 12). This subset targets banks.
- Guidance for prudential supervisors (Principles 13 to 18).

The corporate governance principles in **Figure 10** recommend banks to investigate how climate-related financial risks could impact the resilience of their

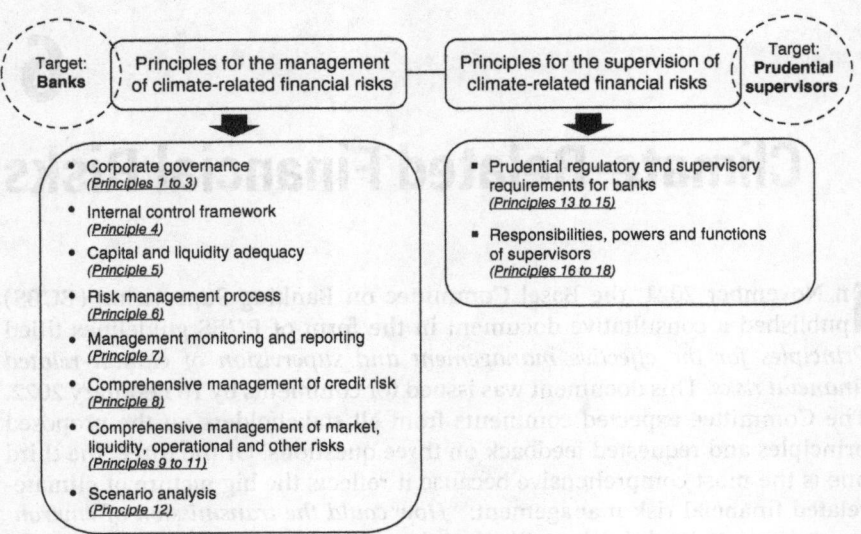

FIGURE 10   Management and supervision of climate-related financial risks

business model, and how these risks may affect their ability to achieve their business objectives. With this aim in mind, banks should embed climate-related financial risks in policies, processes and controls across all relevant functions and business units, inclusive of board members and senior management.

Principle 4 argued that the internal control framework should be structured around three lines of defence. The first line is dedicated to climate-related risk assessments during the client onboarding, credit application and credit review processes. The second and third lines are the risk function and the internal audit function, respectively.

At the core of capital and liquidity adequacy (Principle 5) is the assessment of whether climate-related financial risks could cause net cash outflows or depletion of liquidity buffers. This should be evaluated during both business-as-usual and stressed conditions.

The risk management process (Principle 6) is intended to help the board and senior management of banks to ensure that climate-related financial risks are embedded within the bank's risk appetite framework.[1] This requires defining internal risk limits for the different types of climate-related financial risks to which banks are exposed in the scope of their credit, market, liquidity and operational risk exposures.

Regarding management monitoring and reporting (Principle 7), it is suggested that banks should develop qualitative or quantitative indicators to implement a timely reporting of climate-related financial risks across the banking group, as part of their overall data governance and IT infrastructure. The climate-related financial risk reporting framework should be updated on a regular basis.

Principle 8 focused on the comprehensiveness of credit risk. The main idea is to articulate the bank's credit policies and processes to integrate climate-related financial risks in the entire credit lifecycle. This should include client due diligence and on-going monitoring of clients' risk profiles.

Given the wide scope of the comprehensive management of market, liquidity, operational and other risks, Principles 9 to 11 deal with this issue. In short, banks are urged to

- Identify and understand how climate-related financial risks could impact the value of the financial instruments held in their portfolios.
- Incorporate these impacts into the calibration of liquidity buffers and their liquidity management frameworks.
- Put in place appropriate measures to assess the impact of financial-related risk drivers on the following risks: strategic, reputational and regulatory risk.

The last principle set out by the Basel Committee for the management of climate-related financial risks (Principle 12 in **Figure 10**) prompts banks to use climate scenario analysis. These scenarios should reflect the bank's overall climate risk management objectives as defined by the board and senior management. Some examples of relevant objectives to be included in climate scenario analysis, including stress testing, are provided in BCBS (2021, p. 7):

- Exploring the impact of climate change and the transition to a low-carbon economy on the bank's strategy and the resiliency of its business model.
- Identifying relevant climate-related risk factors.
- Measuring vulnerability to climate-related risks and estimating exposures and potential losses.
- Diagnosing data and methodological limitations in climate risk management.

The second subset of six principles (Principles 13 to 18) is devoted to the supervision of climate-related financial risks (see **Figure 10**) and provides guidance for prudential supervisors.

The three first principles (Principles 13 to 15) are related to prudential regulatory and supervisory requirements for banks. In a nutshell, supervisors are driven to determine that their roles and responsibilities for climate-related financial risks are clearly defined and assigned across the bank. They should also assess the effectiveness of board and senior management oversight of climate-related financial risks (Principle 13).

Another role assigned to supervisors is to assess the extent to which climate-related financial risks are embedded in the bank's business model and global strategy, along with ad hoc procedures to identify, monitor and manage such risks (Principle 14). It is also worth mentioning that supervisors should determine that the scenario analysis and stress testing programmes implemented by banks are commensurate with their size, business model and complexity (Principle 15). This ensures a reliable assessment of a bank's resilience to a range of plausible climate-related outcomes.

Principles 16 to 18 detail the responsibilities, powers and functions of supervisors. Interestingly, they are encouraged to collaborate with a broad and diverse set of stakeholders, including the climate science community, to inform a collective understanding and measurement of climate-related financial risks, and thus allow for optimization of climate-dedicated resources.

NOTE

1. The Financial Stability Board defines risk appetite as *"The aggregate level and types of risk an organization is willing to assume within its risk capacity to achieve its strategic objectives and business plan"*.

Two

The Financial Risk Measurement Landscape

As mentioned in the Introduction to this book, financial risk management in the banking industry is overwhelmed by a plethora of models and methods. Some are readily understandable by non-specialists of financial risk measurement, but the majority are not easily accessible without a solid background in mathematical finance. This second part focuses on the former. Although more technical, this part aims to provide readers with a handy toolbox of risk measurement, the starting point of risk management. Both issues are closely interconnected and thus difficult to disentangle.

Included in this toolbox are the main approaches used to quantify the risk of loss in the banking sector. They can be segmented into two dimensions: empirical and theoretical. The historical approach to risk is built on historically observed data and thus is said to be empirical. The Gaussian and Monte Carlo approaches to risk are grounded on data derived from a theoretical probability distribution.

Once we know the risk of loss, how can we exploit it further? Calculating the risk contributions can add value to a risk estimate, without forgetting the shortcomings of risk metrics, since they are only estimates. This is why it is so important to evaluate ex post the results generated by a risk model. This is called backtesting. From a risk management perspective, we also need to anticipate what happens in a worst-case scenario, such as a stock market crash. What are the maximum losses a bank could experience? Stress testing can answer this question.

## CHAPTER 7

Historical Approach to Risk

STEP-BY-STEP CALCULATION OF HISTORICAL VaR

This approach to risk measurement is grounded in historical simulation and therefore does not require any theoretical probability distribution to compute a risk measure such as Value-at-Risk (VaR) or Expected Shortfall (ES).

Within a historical framework, we will never start a risk calculation with the following statement: *"we assume that the profit and loss of our portfolio follows a Gaussian distribution (or whatever else)"*. There is no distributional assumption about the returns of assets in a portfolio. That is why the historical method is an empirical or nonparametric approach to risk measurement.

It is empirical because it only relies on historical data (observed in the past). It is nonparametric because it does not rely on a theoretical probability distribution specified from parameters such as, for example, the Gaussian distribution. This explains why historical methods are used extensively in financial institutions. As the risk measure is derived from historical returns, there is no bias generated by assuming something wrong about the profit and loss of the portfolio.

To illustrate the historical simulation method, we use a portfolio with two assets for the sake of clarity: Google and Amazon. These two companies belong to the so-called GAFAM and operate in software and computer services, and general retailers, respectively. The historical method is of course extendable to a portfolio with m assets, but a programming language (e.g., Python, R, MATLAB, GAUSS) drastically eases the work. Another option is Excel VBA code (Visual Basic for Applications).[1]

Before running any calculation, it makes sense to identify the market risk factors that impact the value of our Google/Amazon portfolio. Talking about equity portfolios, we can consider the returns of assets as the main market risk factor. A decrease in the stock prices of Google or Amazon will lead to negative returns and the portfolio will thus register a loss. Interestingly, the relationship between these risk factors and the portfolio value is linear (the simplest relationship between two variables).

We also need a dataset of daily historical stock prices for Google and Amazon in order to compute the corresponding historical returns. Usually, but not necessarily, a dataset of 251 stock prices is used to compute 250 historical returns because that corresponds to 1 year of effective trading days on average, depending on the number of national holidays. We thus consider the daily historical stock prices of Google and Amazon from 2021/03/04 to 2022/02/17 (international format: YYYY/MM/DD). The current date is the most recent date in our dataset: 17 February 2022. The current stock prices of Google and Amazon are $2650.78 and $3093.05, respectively. We hold 10 stocks of Google and 20 stocks of Amazon in the portfolio. We consider a long-only portfolio (no short positions).

To assess the risk of this portfolio, we compute a 1-day historical VaR (since we use daily data) at the 99% confidence level. The VaR calculation date is the current date: 17 February 2022. In a nutshell, the historical VaR is an empirical quantile of the portfolio's Profit and Loss (P&L) for a specified confidence level. The historical VaR calculation may be divided into five different steps, each of which should be considered separately. **Figure 11** plots the daily stock prices of Google and Amazon from 2021/03/04 to 2022/02/17. Time on the x-axis is expressed in number of days.

Worked Example 4: Historical VaR Calculation

- *Step 1. Compute historical shocks*

  The historical shocks are the returns of the two assets in the portfolio. Depending on the stock price time evolution observed in the past, returns can be either positive (gain) or negative (loss). They are thus called "shocks". The output of this first step is 250 historical shocks (calculated from 251 prices from 2021/03/04 to 2022/02/17) for Google and Amazon.

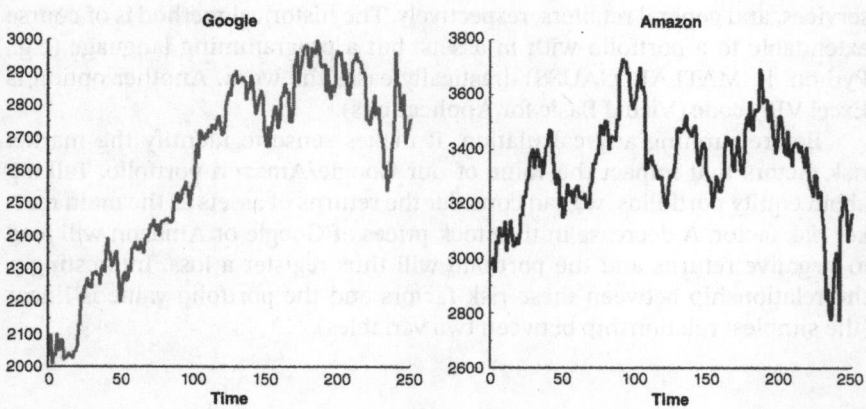

FIGURE 11   Stock prices of Google and Amazon

We have assumed that the market risk factors correspond to the daily stock returns. Let R_t and P_t denote the daily return and price at time t, respectively. They are calculated as follows:

$$R_t = \frac{P_t - P_{t-1}}{P_{t-1}}$$

As an example, the Google historical daily return on 11 February 2022 (#5 in **Table 4**) is

$$R_{2022-02-11} = \frac{P_{2022-02-11} - P_{2022-02-10}}{P_{2022-02-10}} = \frac{2685.65 - 2772.4}{2772.4} = -3.13\%$$

These returns are called simple (or arithmetic) returns. Another option is to calculate log returns (geometric). The daily historical returns of Google and Amazon are reported in **Table 4**. We cannot calculate a historical return on 4 March 2021 (#251 in **Table 4**) because the stock prices the day before (2021-03-03) for Google and Amazon are unavailable in our stock price database. Obviously, with N stock prices, only $N - 1$ returns can be calculated.

- *Step 2. Compute the shocked prices*
    The shocked (or simulated) prices are obtained by applying historical returns to the current price of an asset. This historical simulation process is at the core of the historical VaR method. The idea is to simulate the value of our portfolio by impacting its current value (as of 17 February 2022) by historical shocks observed in the past. The output of this second step is 250 shocked or simulated prices.

TABLE 4   Daily historical returns of Google and Amazon

#	Date	Google	Amazon
		Daily Historical Returns	
1	2022-02-17	-3.77%	-2.18%
2	2022-02-16	0.83%	1.02%
3	2022-02-15	0.80%	0.87%
4	2022-02-14	0.93%	1.22%
5	2022-02-11	-3.13%	-3.59%
6	2022-02-10	-2.10%	-1.36%
7	2022-02-09	1.57%	-0.14%
8	2022-02-08	0.14%	2.20%
9	2022-02-07	-2.86%	0.19%
10	2022-02-04	0.14%	13.54%
...	...	...	...
250	2021-03-05	3.10%	0.77%
251	2021-03-04	NA	NA

At this stage, it is worth mentioning that there is a single current price of each asset in the portfolio ($2650.78 for Google and $3093.05 for Amazon) observed at the current date (17 February 2022). By nature, a current price cannot be time-varying. In contrast, there are 250 time-dependent simulated prices since they are obtained through 250 time-dependent historical returns (Step 1).

We then apply these 250 historical shocks to a single current price observed at a single current date (the present time for us). For example, the shocked or simulated price $P_{s,t}$ of Google on 11 February 2022 (#5 in **Table 5**) is

$$P_{s,t} = P_A \times (1+R_t) = \$2650.78 \times (1+(-3.13\%)) = \$2567.84$$

For Amazon, we obtain

$$P_{s,t} = P_A \times (1+R_t) = \$3093.05 \times (1+(-3.59\%)) = \$2981.97$$

For Google and #10 in **Table 5** (t = 2022-02-04), we have

$$P_{s,t} = P_A \times (1+R_t) = \$2650.78 \times (1+0.14\%) = \$2654.54$$

For Amazon, we obtain

$$P_{s,t} = P_A \times (1+R_t) = \$3093.05 \times (1+13.54\%) = \$3511.72$$

where

$P_{s,t}$ = the shocked price simulated at time t

P_A = the current price observed at the VaR calculation date (17 February 2022) and thus not time-varying

R_t = the historical return (market risk factor) at time t

We report in **Table 5** the first ten and last two shocked prices of Google and Amazon.

- **Step 3. Compute the portfolio P&L**

The P&L of the portfolio is defined as the difference between its simulated or shocked value and its current value:

$$P\&L = \underbrace{\text{Simulated value}}_{\substack{\text{Calculated for each} \\ \text{historical date of the} \\ \text{dataset } (N = 250)}} - \underbrace{\text{Current value}}_{\substack{\text{Observed at the current date:} \\ \text{17 February 2022 } (N = 1)}}$$

where N is the number of observations.

TABLE 5   Shocked prices of Google and Amazon

		Shocked prices ($)	
#	Date	Google	Amazon
1	2022-02-17	2550.72	3025.59
2	2022-02-16	2672.70	3124.47
3	2022-02-15	2671.95	3119.83
4	2022-02-14	2675.33	3130.85
5	2022-02-11	2567.84	2981.97
6	2022-02-10	2595.14	3051.10
7	2022-02-09	2692.48	3088.76
8	2022-02-08	2654.55	3161.16
9	2022-02-07	2575.08	3098.86
10	2022-02-04	2654.54	3511.72
...	...	...	...
250	2021-03-05	2733.07	3116.83
251	2021-03-04	NA	NA

Here, we work at the portfolio level and not at the asset level as in Step 2. As a result, we have to include both the number of Google and Amazon stocks and the long/short positions held on each asset in our P&L calculation. As a reminder, we hold 10 stocks of Google and 20 stocks of Amazon and our portfolio is long-only. The output of this third step is 250 P&L values obtained from the 250 simulated prices calculated in Step 2. For example, the portfolio P&L for $t = 2022\text{-}02\text{-}11$ (#5 in **Table 6**) is

$$\text{P\&L} = \underbrace{[(10 \times \$2567.84) + (20 \times \$2981.97)]}_{\substack{\text{Portfolio simulated value} \\ = \\ \text{Number of stocks} \times \text{Shocked stock price}}} - \underbrace{[(10 \times \$2650.78) + (20 \times \$3093.05)]}_{\substack{\text{Current portfolio value (2022-02-17)} \\ = \\ \text{Number of stocks} \times \text{Current stock price}}} = -\$3050.94$$

We report in **Table 6** the first ten and last two portfolio P&Ls. The historical (or empirical) frequencies of Google and Amazon's daily returns are plotted in **Figure 12**. We also graph the empirical distribution of the portfolio P&L. As shown, these three distributions are far from the perfect Gaussian bell-shaped curve.

TABLE 6   Simulated portfolio P&L

	Portfolio P&L ($)	
#	Date	P&L ($)
1	2022-02-17	-2349.67
2	2022-02-16	847.62
3	2022-02-15	747.35
4	2022-02-14	1001.51
5	2022-02-11	-3050.94
6	2022-02-10	-1395.33
7	2022-02-09	331.17
8	2022-02-08	1399.99
9	2022-02-07	-640.82
10	2022-02-04	8411.05
...	...	...
250	2021-03-05	1298.45
251	2021-03-04	NA

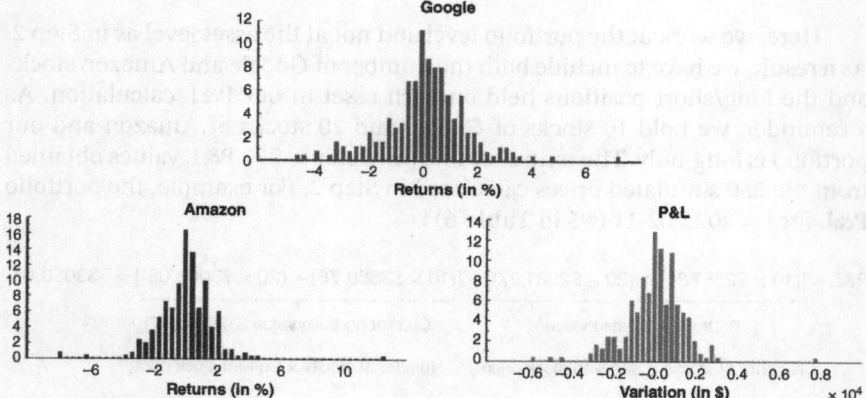

FIGURE 12   Empirical distributions of Google and Amazon returns and the portfolio P&L

- *Step 4. Order statistics*

    The idea of order statistics is very intuitive because they are sample values sorted in ascending order. To get the order statistics, there is nothing to calculate. From Step 3, we have a sample of 250 simulated P&L values sorted by historical dates, from the most recent: 17 February 2022 (the current date) to the oldest: 4 March 2021. If we put these 250 P&L

values in numerical increasing order, we get the order statistics of the P&L distribution:

$$\min P\&L = P\&L_{1:n} \leq P\&L_{2:n} \leq \cdots \leq P\&L_{n-1:n} \leq P\&L_{n:n} = \max P\&L$$

where min/max P&L denotes the lowest/highest numerical P&L values, and n is the sample size (250 P&L sample values).

Order statistics are denoted by $P\&L_{i:n}$ and we identify the ith-order statistic or equivalently the statistic of order i in a sample of n observations. As an example, $P\&L_{10:250}$ is the 10th-order statistic of our P&L distribution (or the P&L statistic of order 10), that is the 10th lowest P&L value in the sample of 250 P&L values. The two extreme order statistics are $P\&L_{1:250}$ and $P\&L_{250:250}$, which correspond to the minimal and maximal P&L values, respectively. The former will probably be a loss unless you are a very efficient and lucky portfolio manager, and the latter should hopefully be a profit because you cannot always lose money.

Table 7 displays the order statistics of the portfolio P&L distribution. Each one corresponds to a P&L value sorted in ascending order (column P&L (\$)↑ in the table). The order statistics range from the first-order statistic $P\&L_{1:250}$, the lowest numerical value (the P&L worst-case scenario since this is the highest loss) to the last-order statistic $P\&L_{250:250}$, the highest numerical value (the highest profit historically experienced).

TABLE 7   Order statistics

#	Date	P&L (\$)↑	Order Statistics
11	2022-02-03	−5712.47	$P\&L_{1:250}$
145	2021-07-30	−4884.90	$P\&L_{2:250}$
20	2022-01-21	−4268.64	$P\&L_{3:250}$
5	2022-02-11	−3050.94	$P\&L_{4:250}$
241	2021-03-18	−2900.51	$P\&L_{5:250}$
18	2022-01-25	−2734.77	$P\&L_{6:250}$
103	2021-09-28	−2616.79	$P\&L_{7:250}$
85	2021-10-22	−2598.16	$P\&L_{8:250}$
204	2021-05-10	−2578.67	$P\&L_{9:250}$
32	2022-01-05	−2384.82	$P\&L_{10:250}$
. . .	. . .	. . .	. . .
10	2022-02-04	8411.05	$P\&L_{250:250}$
251	2021-03-04	NA	NA

■ *Step 5. Compute the empirical quantile of the portfolio P&L*

The output of this last step is the historical VaR. We know that we are looking for a specific value of our portfolio P&L called the quantile and calculated for a user-specified (or set by the regulator) confidence level. We thus need a generic definition of this quantile to get the historical VaR. Let VaR^H denote the historical VaR. Then VaR_α^H equals the $n \times (1 - \alpha)$ *i*th lowest value of the portfolio P&L. Therefore, we are looking for the order statistic (see Step 4) denoted $P\&L_{n\times(1-\alpha):n}$.

In our example, $n = 250$ and the confidence level α is 99%. We thus have

$$n \times (1 - \alpha) = 250 \times (1 - 99\%) = 2.5$$

The order statistic of interest is $P\&L_{2.5:250}$, that is the 2.5th lowest value of the 250 portfolio P&L values. Of course, this order statistic does not exist. However, we know the second- and third-order statistics ($P\&L_{2:250}$ and $P\&L_{3:250}$) of the portfolio P&L distribution. We can use these two order statistics to calculate $P\&L_{2.5:250}$ through a linear interpolation. We have the following generic definition for the historical VaR:

$$VaR_\alpha^H = P\&L_{n^*:n} + \left(n \times \left(1 - \alpha\right) - n^*\right)\left(P\&L_{n^*+1:n} - P\&L_{n^*:n}\right)$$

where n^* is the inferior integer part of $n \times (1 - \alpha)$.

Using data in **Table 7**, VaR^H is computed as follows:

$$VaR_{99\%}^H = P\&L_{n^*:n} + \left(n \times \left(1 - \alpha\right) - n^*\right)\left(P\&L_{n^*+1:n} - P\&L_{n^*:n}\right)$$

$$= P\&L_{2:250} + 0.5\left(P\&L_{3:250} - P\&L_{2:250}\right)$$

$$= -4884.90 + 0.5\left(-4268.64 - \left(-4884.90\right)\right)$$

$$VaR_{99\%}^H = -\$4576.77$$

We can check that $VaR_{99\%}^H$ ranges between $P\&L_{2:250}$ and $P\&L_{3:250}$ due to the interpolation scheme. It is common practice to disclose the absolute value of a VaR result. The 1-day historical VaR of our Google/Amazon portfolio at the 99% confidence level is thus \$4576.77.

UNDERSTANDING A VaR RESULT

We can draw the following conclusion from our risk calculation: over the next 24 hours, the probability of incurring a loss higher than \$4576.77 is 1%. Equivalently, the probability of incurring a loss lower than or equal to \$4576.77 is 99%.

The time horizon is 24 hours because we have calculated a 1-day VaR (daily data for Google and Amazon). The probability of 99% corresponds to the confidence level we have specified, and $1 - 99\% = 1\%$ is the risk of being wrong (or the error risk).

What is really relevant in terms of risk management is the 1% and not the 99%. The true risk lies in the 1% of the worst portfolio P&L outcomes (the 1% highest losses), not in the 99% where the worst-case scenario is a potential loss equal to the VaR. This 99% risk can be hedged, but what happens if the actual loss is hugely more than $4576.77? Such a loss could severely impact the financial resilience of a bank.

The VaR is seductive but dangerous, because it is nothing more than an estimated maximal loss a portfolio can potentially incur over a given time horizon, for a theoretical confidence level. The VaR is definitely unable to predict the future. The golden rule is never to expect more than the VaR can give: a rough estimate of your risk exposure within 24 hours.

In order to comply with the backtesting rules set by the Basel Committee on Banking Supervision (BCBS), we need to compute a 10-day VaR. With this aim, we use the square-root-of-time rule (also called scaling) to translate the 1-day VaR into a 10-day VaR. This rule indicates that

$$\text{10-day VaR}_\alpha^H = \text{1-day VaR}_\alpha \times \sqrt{10}$$

With our Google/Amazon portfolio, we obtain

$$\text{10-day VaR}_{99\%}^H = \text{1-day VaR}_{99\%}^H \times \sqrt{10} = \$4576.77 \times \sqrt{10} = \$14,473.02$$

The previous VaR interpretation holds true. The only change is an increased time horizon from 1 to 10 days. From a regulatory viewpoint (BCBS), a 10-day is more interesting than a 1-day risk estimate because the risk capital requirement (the capital charge for different types of risk) is higher. In terms of risk management, we say that a 10-day risk estimate is more conservative than its 1-day counterpart.

THE WORST MISTAKE YOU CAN MAKE

We hold a two-asset portfolio and want to calculate its historical VaR. Why not calculate the VaR of Google and the VaR of Amazon, and then add both individual VaRs to get the portfolio VaR?

Because it is totally wrong, except in a purely theoretical situation. Let's calculate these two VaRs to understand why. Following the same Steps 1 to 5 used to compute the portfolio VaR, we obtain the following results at the 99% confidence level:

$$\text{Google 1-day VaR}^{H}_{99\%} = -1132.20 + 0.5(-1000.55 - (-1132.20))$$
$$= -\$1066.38$$
$$\text{Amazon 1-day VaR}^{H}_{99\%} = -4679.72 + 0.5(-3680.85 - (-4679.72))$$
$$= -\$4180.28$$

Thus

$$\text{Portfolio 1-day VaR}^{H}_{99\%} = \text{Google 1-day VaR}^{H}_{99\%} + \text{Amazon 1-day VaR}^{H}_{99\%}$$
$$= -\$1066.38 + (-\$4180.28) = -\$5246.66$$

If we report the two $\text{VaR}^{H}_{99\%}$s in absolute value, the 1-day $\text{VaR}^{H}_{99\%}$ computed by summing the two individual VaRs ($5246.66) is higher than the 1-day $\text{VaR}^{H}_{99\%}$ computed from the portfolio P&L ($4576.77). Here is the big mistake. The former VaR calculation implicitly assumes that the correlation between Google and Amazon daily returns is equal to one. Stated differently, there is no risk reduction when structuring a portfolio with both Google and Amazon against holding two one-asset portfolios. This holds true only when the correlation between two asset returns equals +1. Under this purely theoretical scenario, we know that diversification does not lead to any risk reduction. Putting all your eggs in one basket, or two different baskets, will lead to the same risk level.

A salient property of the correlation coefficient is to be bounded between +1 and −1 inclusive. Interestingly, each bound is easily interpretable in terms of risk management. The upper bound (+1) indicates there is no risk reduction when two asset returns are perfectly positively correlated. This is the exact opposite with the lower bound (−1). When two asset returns are perfectly negatively correlated, the risk reduction is maximal. Therefore, there is a risk reduction once the correlation is different from one.

The correlation between Google and Amazon's daily returns is equal to 52.82%, which is obviously different from +1 or 100%. As a result, from a risk management standpoint, it makes sense to include both Google and Amazon in the same portfolio. As their daily returns are not perfectly positively correlated, we will reduce the risk of our portfolio. The difference between the portfolio VaR and the sum of the two individual VaRs is called the diversification gain. The negative sign indicates a risk decrease:

$$\text{Diversification gain} = \$4576.77 - \$5246.66 = -\$669.9$$

DO YOU SPEAK MARK-TO-MARKET?

In mark-to-market, the price of an asset is marked to the current market price. It is an accounting method that helps to measure the fair/reasonable value of assets. The Mark-to-Market (MtM) of a portfolio is calculated with respect to the current market prices. The MtM of our Google/Amazon portfolio is thus

$$\text{MtM} = (10 \times \$2650.78) + (20 \times \$3093.05) = \$88\,368.80$$

Number of Google stocks ×
Current Google stock price (as of 2022-02-17)

Number of Amazon stocks ×
Current Amazon stock price (as of 2022-02-17)

We can compute the shocked (or simulated) MtM_s of our portfolio from the shocked (or simulated) stock prices of Google and Amazon. For example, the MtM_s for $t = $ 2022-02-11 is

$$\text{MtM}_s = (10 \times \$2567.84) + (20 \times \$2981.97) = \$85\,317.86$$

Number of Google stocks ×
Shocked or simulated Google stock price (as of 2022-02-17)

Number of Amazon stocks ×
Shocked or simulated Amazon stock price (as of 2022-02-17)

With the resulting 250 simulated MtM values, we compute the 250 portfolio P&L outcomes as in Step 3. The portfolio value at time t is still equal to the difference between the portfolio simulated value at time t and the portfolio current value (2022-02-17). As before, MtM_s is time-varying and MtM is not time-dependent since it is a current value. For $t = $ 2022-02-11, we find the same P&L value as in **Table 6**:

$$\text{P\&L} = \text{MtM}_s - \text{MtM} = -\$3050.94$$

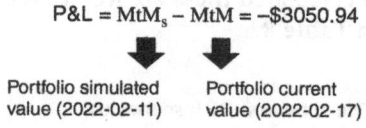

Portfolio simulated value (2022-02-11)

Portfolio current value (2022-02-17)

The VaR calculation, strictly speaking, is not altered in any way when using MtM. We average the second- and third-order statistics of the portfolio P&L in **Table 7** and obtain the historical VaR as in Step 5 (−$4576.77).

BEYOND VaR

Under the Basel III regulatory framework, VaR at the 99% confidence level is replaced by ES at the 97.5% level. However, the daily VaR with a 99% confidence level and a sample of the last 250 observations is still used by the regulator for backtesting purposes. Both risk measures are closely related, since ES is simply the expected loss beyond the VaR for a given confidence level α:

$$ES_\alpha = \mathbb{E}[\text{Loss}|\text{Loss} \geq \text{VaR}_\alpha]$$

ES is thus a more conservative risk measure than VaR, since it is greater or equal than VaR for a given confidence level α. The above equation also indicates that ES is equal to the expected loss given that loss is beyond the VaR. It follows that ES is calculated by averaging the $n \times (1-\alpha)$ first-order statistics of the portfolio P&L, where n and α denote the number of P&L sample values and the confidence level, respectively.

Worked Example 5: Historical ES Calculation

We still work with a sample of 250 historically simulated P&L values (as for the historical VaR) but the confidence level is no longer 99% but 97.5% instead. We thus have

$$n \times (1-\alpha) = 250 \times (1-0.975) = 6.25$$

As 6.25 is not an integer, we cannot identify the portfolio P&L order statistics required to compute the ES. To fix that problem, we use n^*, the inferior integer part of $n \times (1-\alpha)$, as we did for the historical VaR calculation (Step 5). We have $n^* = 6$. Under the Basel III regulatory framework, computing the historical ES is then equivalent to averaging the six worst P&Ls of the 250 historical scenarios. We have calculated these six worst P&L scenarios in **Table 7**. They are reproduced in **Table 8**.

TABLE 8 The six worst P&L scenarios

#	Date	P&L ($) ↑	Order statistic
11	2022-02-03	-5712.47	$P\&L_{1:250}$
145	2021-07-30	-4884.90	$P\&L_{2:250}$
20	2022-01-21	-4268.64	$P\&L_{3:250}$
5	2022-02-11	-3050.94	$P\&L_{4:250}$
241	2021-03-18	-2900.51	$P\&L_{5:250}$
18	2022-01-25	-2734.77	$P\&L_{6:250}$

Averaging the six first-order statistics of the P&L (taken in absolute value), we obtain the 97.5% ES:

$$\text{ES}^{\text{H}}_{97.5\%} = \frac{1}{6} \times \left(5712.47 + 4884.90 + 4268.64 + 3050.94 + 2900.51 + 2734.77 \right)$$

$$= \$3925.37$$

It is not relevant to compare ES and VaR when the confidence level of ES is lower than the confidence level of VaR. This explains why we cannot compare the ES at 97.5% (Basel III) with the VaR at 99% (Basel I and II). We can check that the ES is more conservative than the VaR for the same confidence level:

$$\text{ES}^{\text{H}}_{99\%} = \$5298.69 > \text{VaR}^{\text{H}}_{99\%} = \$4576.77$$

We now have two risk measures for our Google/Amazon portfolio:

The 1-day historical VaR at the 99% level: $\text{VaR}^{\text{H}}_{99\%} = \$4576.77$

The 1-day historical ES at the 97.5% level: $\text{ES}^{\text{H}}_{97.5\%} = \$3925.37$

The VaR tells us that the probability of incurring a potential maximal loss of \$4576.77 over the next 24 hours is equal to 1%. Although an estimate, this is the most relevant risk information.

The ES indicates how much we could lose on average over the next 24 hours with our Google/Amazon portfolio if an extreme event (with a very low probability of occurrence but a huge impact) should occur. The ES is the mean of losses beyond a given confidence level. Therefore, over the next 24 hours, the probability of our Google/Amazon portfolio experiencing an average loss of \$3925.37 is equal to 2.5%. This is still nothing more than an estimate.

NOTE

1. Of course, it is possible to calculate a risk metric such as VaR and ES for a portfolio of *m* assets. Portfolios of two assets are not usual in practice. However, this requires matrix calculation – a domain of mathematics used extensively in financial risk management but beyond the scope of this book.

## CHAPTER 8

The Gaussian Framework

THE CORE EQUATION

This is the most convenient solution to compute both the Value-at-Risk (VaR) and Expected Shortfall (ES). Under this framework, we compute a Gaussian VaR and ES, grounded on a wrong but handy assumption about the portfolio Profit and Loss (P&L). We assume that it follows a Gaussian (or normal) distribution. Actually, this assumption is neither totally wrong nor totally right. In other words, each time we compute a Gaussian VaR and ES, we know we are mistaken. We can thus wonder why the Gaussian framework is still used by portfolio or risk managers, specifically to assess the risk of equities portfolios.

The main reason is that the Gaussian framework is mathematically tractable, especially when the portfolio P&L is a linear function of the asset returns. We can derive a closed-form expression of the Gaussian VaR and ES that is easy to manipulate, expressed as the product of a (theoretical) quantile and the portfolio volatility (if we omit the term of expected returns). This explains why the Gaussian VaR is an analytical risk measure.[1]

The Gaussian VaR and ES are two parametric risk measures because they are defined from the two parameters of a Gaussian distribution: the mean and the standard deviation. The former refers to the average asset returns and the latter refers to the portfolio volatility. The Gaussian VaR and ES are thus two standard-deviation risk measures. More generally speaking, each time a risk measure is grounded on a distributional assumption, it is known as parametric.[2] In this chapter, we are going to compute a Gaussian parametric VaR and ES. At the core of this method is the covariance (or variance–covariance) matrix, which calculates the variances and covariances of assets for VaR calculation. The variance–covariance method is also called the model-building approach.

Worked Example 6: Gaussian VaR Calculation

Assuming that our Google/Amazon portfolio follows a Gaussian distribution: $P\&L \sim \mathcal{N}(\mu(P\&L), \sigma(P\&L))$, the closed-form formula of the Gaussian VaR, denoted VaR_α^G, is the following:

$$VaR_\alpha^G = -\mu(P\&L) + \Phi^{-1}(\alpha) \times \sigma(P\&L)$$

where

- $\mu(P\&L)$ is the expected return of the portfolio expressed in terms of P&L.
- $\Phi^{-1}(\alpha)$ is the inverse cumulative density function (cdf) of the standardized Gaussian distribution for the α confidence level. In short, this is the theoretical quantile we need to compute the Gaussian VaR.
- $\sigma(P\&L)$ is the standard deviation or volatility of the portfolio expressed in terms of P&L.

In order to compute the Gaussian VaR and ES, additional data are required: the daily volatilities and average returns of Google and Amazon stocks. These data can be derived directly from the dataset used to compute the historical VaR (**Table 4**):

- $\mu_G = 0.1177\%$ is the average daily return of Google
- $\mu_A = 0.0319\%$ is the average daily return of Amazon
- $\sigma_G = 1.5309\%$ is the daily volatility (standard deviation) of Google
- $\sigma_A = 1.8362\%$ is the daily volatility (standard deviation) of Amazon

As a reminder, the correlation between the two asset returns is 52.8189%.

THE COVARIANCE MATRIX

As mentioned before, the big deal with the Gaussian VaR calculation is the covariance matrix, which is used extensively in risk management. The covariance matrix is a *generalization* of the variance. This matrix is both square (same number of rows and columns) and symmetric (elements above and below its diagonal are equal).[3] With two assets in the portfolio, the covariance matrix is straightforward to calculate since its size (number of rows × number of columns) equals $2 \times 2 = 4$ elements. It is called a square matrix of order 4, or a fourth-order square matrix. With m assets in the portfolio, we have the following expression for the variance–covariance matrix (the shortcut "covariance matrix" is frequently used):

$$
\underset{(m \times m)}{\text{VCM}} = \overset{j \rightarrow}{\underset{i \downarrow}{\begin{pmatrix} \sigma_1^2 & \cdots & \sigma_{1m} \\ \vdots & \ddots & \vdots \\ \sigma_{m1} & \cdots & \sigma_m^2 \end{pmatrix}}}
$$

To identify an element within this matrix, we list the row number i then the column number j. The variances $\sigma_1^2, \cdots, \sigma_m^2$ of each asset in the portfolio are displayed on the diagonal of the covariance matrix. The covariances $\sigma_{ij} = \sigma_{ji}$ are reported on either side of this diagonal. The covariance matrix of our Google (G)/Amazon (A) portfolio is written as follows:

$$
\text{VCM} = \begin{pmatrix} \sigma_G^2 & \sigma_{G,A} \\ \sigma_{A,G} & \sigma_A^2 \end{pmatrix}
$$

Although the portfolio covariance matrix includes four elements, only three calculations are required since the covariance between Google and Amazon returns $\left(\sigma_{G,A}\right)$ is equal to the covariance between Amazon and Google returns $\left(\sigma_{A,G}\right)$.

The point is that we do not know the covariance between the two asset returns, but their correlation. Thankfully, there is a relationship between covariance and correlation that allows us to calculate the former from the latter and vice versa:[4]

$$
\rho_{G,A} = \frac{\sigma_{G,A}}{\sigma_G \times \sigma_A}
$$

where

- $\rho_{G,A}$ is the correlation coefficient between Google and Amazon returns.
- $\sigma_{G,A}$ is the covariance between Google and Amazon returns.
- σ_G and σ_A are the respective volatilities of Google and Amazon (standard deviations).

Since we are interested in the covariance, we can rewrite the correlation formula $\rho_{G,A}$ as

$$
\sigma_{G,A} = \rho_{G,A} \times \sigma_G \times \sigma_A
$$

With the numerical values, we deduce that

$$\sigma_{G,A} = 52.8189\% \times 1.5309\% \times 1.8362\% = 0.0148\%$$

The variance is equal to the square of the standard deviation. Thus, for Google and Amazon:

$$\sigma_G^2 = \left(1.5309\%\right)^2 = 0.0234\%$$

$$\sigma_A^2 = \left(1.8362\%\right)^2 = 0.0337\%$$

Finally, the covariance matrix of our Google/Amazon portfolio is

$$\underset{(2 \times 2)}{\text{VCM}} = \begin{pmatrix} \sigma_G^2 & \sigma_{G,A} \\ \sigma_{A,G} & \sigma_A^2 \end{pmatrix} \quad \blacktriangleright \quad \text{VCM} = \begin{pmatrix} 0.0234\% & 0.0148\% \\ 0.0148\% & 0.0337\% \end{pmatrix}$$

Equivalently, we can define the portfolio variance σ_P^2 without a matrix:

$$\sigma_P^2 = \sigma_G^2 + \sigma_A^2 + 2 \times \sigma_{G,A}$$

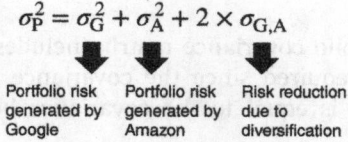

Portfolio risk generated by Google   Portfolio risk generated by Amazon   Risk reduction due to diversification

Calculating the sum of the four elements of the covariance matrix, or using the σ_P^2 equation, returns exactly the same output: the Google/Amazon portfolio variance, since σ_P^2 calculates the sum of the four elements of VCM. Thus

$$\sigma_P^2 = 0.0234\% + 0.0337\% + (2 \times 0.0148\%) = \underline{0.0868\%}$$

Sum of the four elements of the Google/Amazon portfolio covariance matrix (VCM)

This portfolio variance is expressed as a percentage, but we need a portfolio volatility $\sigma(\text{P\&L})$ expressed in terms of the P&L (value, or $), as indicated in the Gaussian VaR formula

$$\text{VaR}_\alpha^G = -\mu(\text{P\&L}) + \Phi^{-1}(\alpha) \times \sigma(\text{P\&L})$$

To do this, we must integrate into the portfolio variance calculation both the current value (as of 17 February 2022), that is the mark-to-market of Google and Amazon. We have calculated MtM_G (Google) and MtM_A (Amazon) to compute the historical VaR:

- $\text{MtM}_G = 10 \times \$2650.78 = \$26\,507.80$
- $\text{MtM}_A = 20 \times \$3093.05 = \$61\,861.00$

The portfolio variance $\sigma^2(\text{P\&L})$ (value, or \$) is calculated as follows:

$$\sigma^2\left(\text{P\&L}\right) = \sigma^2\left(R_G\right) + \text{MtM}_G^2 + \sigma^2\left(R_A\right) + \text{MtM}_A^2$$
$$+ 2 \times \sigma\left(R_G, R_A\right) \times \text{MtM}_G \times \text{MtM}_A$$

where

- $\sigma^2\left(R_G\right)$ and $\sigma^2\left(R_A\right)$ are the variances of the daily returns of Google and Amazon.
- MtM_G and MtM_A are the mark-to-market of Google and Amazon, that is the current value or nominal exposure (as of 17 February 2022), calculated as number of stocks × current price.
- $\sigma\left(R_G, R_A\right)$ is the covariance between the daily returns of Google and Amazon.

It is worth noting that we are still computing the sum of the four elements of our Google/Amazon portfolio covariance matrix, but this time expressed in terms of P&L (value, or \$) and not as a percentage as we did before with σ_P^2. With the numerical values, we obtain

$$\sigma^2(\text{P\&L}) = (0.0234\%)^2 \times (\$26\,507.80)^2 + (0.0337\%)^2 \times (61\,861.0)^2$$
$$+ 2 \times 0.0148\% \times \$26\,507.80 \times \$61\,861.0$$

$$= \underbrace{\$1\,941\,886.27}$$

Sum of the four elements of the
Google/Amazon portfolio covariance
matrix (VCM)

Then, we simply take the square root of $\sigma^2(\text{P\&L})$ to get the portfolio volatility term $\sigma(\text{P\&L})$ in the Gaussian VaR equation:

$$\sigma(\text{P\&L}) = \sqrt{\$1\,941\,886.27} = \$1393.52$$

The portfolio volatility expressed in terms of profit and loss indicates that the daily change in value (\$) of the Google/Amazon portfolio is \$1393.52. This is the portfolio standard deviation expressed in value (in monetary units), in contrast to the same portfolio volatility expressed as a percentage ($\sigma_p = 2.9470\%$). The volatility of a portfolio, calculated as the standard deviation, can be expressed both in value and in percentage terms.[5]

THE QUANTILE OF THE STANDARDIZED GAUSSIAN DISTRIBUTION

The term $\Phi^{-1}(\alpha)$ in the VaR_α^G equation denotes the quantile of the standardized normal distribution – a special case of the normal distribution when a normal random variable has a mean of zero and a standard deviation of one.

A quantile is calculated for a given confidence level α, for example 99%, and its value depends only on this confidence level. Statistically speaking, we call the quantile of order α (with $\alpha \in [0, 1]$) of a probability distribution $\mathcal{D}$, the real number denoted as z_α, such that, if X is a random variable following a distribution $\mathcal{D}$, we have $P\left(X \leq z_\alpha\right) = \alpha$.

The quantile function is also known as the inverse cdf. In non-technical language, a quantile defines a particular part of a dataset. Put differently, a quantile determines how many values in a distribution are above or below a certain limit.[6]

In the term $\Phi^{-1}(\alpha)$, the Greek capital letter "Phi" stands for the cdf of the standardized normal (or Gaussian) distribution. The exponent -1 indicates the inverse cdf, that is the quantile function of the standardized normal distribution. In contrast to the empirical quantile used to compute the historical VaR_α^H, the term $\Phi^{-1}(\alpha)$ denotes a theoretical quantile since it is defined from a theoretical probability distribution (the normal or Gaussian distribution).

The calculation of $\Phi^{-1}(\alpha)$ is simpler than its definition. As we aim to determine the Gaussian VaR at the 99% confidence level, we need $\Phi^{-1}(99\%)$. Two equivalent statistical functions of Excel return the inverse of the standard normal cumulative distribution:

- NORM.INV(probability, mean, standard_dev)
  Within the brackets are the three arguments of the NORM.INV function: probability is the confidence level α, mean is the average of the distribution and standard_dev is the standard deviation of the distribution. As we work with the standardized normal distribution (mean

TABLE 9 Inverse cdf of the standardized normal distribution for different α

α	99.99%	99.9%	99%	97.5%	95%	90%
Φ_α^{-1}	3.7190	3.0902	2.3263	1.9600	1.6449	1.2816

of zero and standard deviation of one), we input NORM.INV(0.99, 0, 1) and obtain $\Phi^{-1}(99\%) = 2.3263$.

- NORM.S.INV(probability)

    This function requires a single argument since the letter S means "standardized" and Excel then understands that you are talking about the standardized normal (Gaussian) distribution: NORM.S.INV(0.99) returns $\Phi^{-1}(99\%) = 2.3263$.

For a standardized normal distribution, the 99th percentile is 2.3263 since $P\left(z_{99\%} \leq 2.3263\right) = 0.99$. The most useful $\Phi^{-1}(\alpha)$ values in risk management are reported in **Table 9**. We see that the higher the quantile, the more conservative the VaR. This explains why the regulators set high confidence levels for risk measures computation (99% for VaR and 97.5% for ES). The capital charge for financial institutions mechanically increases.

THE EXPECTED RETURN TERM

It is common practice to omit the expected return term μ(P&L) in the Gaussian VaR formula, meaning we assume it equals zero. This assumption is not a big deal for the minimum holding period of the VaR (10 trading days after applying the square-root-of-time rule or scaling). Over this short time horizon, it can be shown that the impact of the expected return term, when compared to the volatility term, can be considered negligible on the end result of the VaR. Moreover, in practice, it is very difficult to estimate the mean, and we assume μ(P&L) = 0.[7] To stay in line with the VaR_α^G equation, we include the expected return term in our VaR calculation. We thus need the average daily returns of Google (μ_G) and Amazon (μ_A):

- $\mu_G = 0.1177\%$
- $\mu_A = 0.0319\%$

With μ_G and μ_A, we can compute the expected return term $\mu(P\&L)$ in the Gaussian VaR equation. First, we calculate both asset returns expressed in value (\$):

$$\text{Google: } \mu_G(\text{in \$}) = \mu_G(\text{in \%}) \times \underbrace{\text{Current value (2022-02-17)}}_{\underbrace{\text{Number of stocks} \times \text{Current price (2022-02-17)}}_{10 \times \$2650.78 = \$26\,507.80}}$$

$$= 0.1177\% \times \$26\,507.80 = \$31.20$$

$$\text{Amazon: } \mu_A(\text{in \$}) = \mu_A(\text{in \%}) \times \underbrace{\text{Current value (2022-02-17)}}_{\underbrace{\text{Number of stocks} \times \text{Current price (2022-02-17)}}_{20 \times \$3093.05 = \$61\,861.0}}$$

$$= 0.0319\% \times \$61\,861.0 = \$19.75$$

Therefore, the expected return term of the Google/Amazon portfolio is

$$\mu(P\&L) = \mu_G(\$) + \mu_A(\$)$$
$$= \$31.20 + \$19.75$$
$$= \$50.95$$

THE GAUSSIAN VaR

Now that we know the three components of the 1-day Gaussian VaR, we can compute it:

$$\text{VaR}_{99\%}^G = -\mu(P\&L) + \Phi^{-1}(99\%) \times \sigma(P\&L)$$

$$= -\$50.95 + 2.3263 \times \$1393.52$$

$$= \$3190.85$$

Another way to compute the Gaussian VaR is to use the portfolio volatility expressed as a percentage ($\sigma_p = 2.9470\%$) instead of expressed in value ($\sigma(P\&L) = \$1393.52$). With this aim, we must integrate the weight of both assets in the portfolio into the VaR calculation. Let w_G and w_A be the weights of Google and Amazon in the portfolio. We deduce that

$$w_G = \frac{\text{MtM}_G}{\text{MtM}_P} = \frac{\$26\,507.80}{\$88\,368.80} = 30.0\%$$

$$w_A = \frac{\text{MtM}_A}{\text{MtM}_P} = \frac{\$61\,861.00}{\$88\,368.80} = 70.0\%$$

where MtM_P is the mark-to-market of the portfolio:

$$\text{MtM}_P = \text{MtM}_G + \text{MtM}_A$$

$$= \$26\,507.80 + \$61\,861.00 = \$88\,368.80$$

We note that the sum of weights is always equal to 100%.
The portfolio variance σ_P^2 is then defined as follows:

$$\sigma_P^2 = w_G^2 \times \sigma^2\left(R_G\right) + w_A^2 \times \sigma^2\left(R_A\right) + 2 \times \sigma\left(R_G, R_A\right) \times w_G \times w_A$$

$$= 30\%^2 \times 0.0234\% + 70\%^2 \times 0.0337\% + 2 \times 0.0148\% \times 30\% \times 70\%$$

$$= 0.0249\%$$

where

- $\sigma^2\left(R_G\right)$ and $\sigma^2\left(R_A\right)$ are the variances of the daily returns of Google (G) and Amazon (A) expressed as a percentage.
- $\sigma\left(R_G, R_A\right)$ is the covariance between the daily returns of Google and Amazon.

The portfolio volatility σ_P is thus equal to

$$\sigma_P = \sqrt{0.0249\%} = 1.5769\%$$

Finally, we deduce that the 1-day Gaussian VaR is equal to

$$\text{VaR}_{99\%}^G = -\mu(\text{P\&L}) + \Phi^{-1}(99\%) \times \sigma_P \times \text{MtM}_P$$

$$= -\$50.95 + 2.3263 \times 1.5769\% \times \$88\,368.80$$

$$= \$3190.85$$

Of course, we obtain the same Gaussian VaR that we got with the portfolio volatility expressed in value, $\sigma(P\&L)$. As for any VaR calculation, regardless of the method used, we can compute a 10-day Gaussian VaR by using the square-root-of-time rule:

$$10\text{-day } VaR_{99\%}^{G} = 1\text{-day } VaR_{\alpha}^{G} \times \sqrt{10}$$

$$= \$3190.85 \times \sqrt{10} = \$10\,090.16$$

It is interesting to compare the two VaRs calculated with the same Google/Amazon portfolio:

- Historical VaR $\rightarrow VaR_{99\%}^{H} = \$4576.77$
- Gaussian VaR $\rightarrow VaR_{99\%} = \$3190.85$

Unsurprisingly, the Gaussian VaR is lower than the historical VaR. We know that under the Gaussian framework, the portfolio P&L is assumed to follow a Gaussian distribution, which is perfectly symmetric (skewness equals zero) and without fat tails (kurtosis equals three).[8] The reality of financial markets tells a different story. All asset return distributions are asymmetric and display fat tails. As a result, the Gaussian assumption leads to an underestimated probability of loss occurrence in the tails – where the risk is truly dangerous for the bank – resulting in an underestimated VaR.

We can also express both the historical and Gaussian VaR as a percentage of the portfolio value. We obtain a relative VaR:

$$VaR_{\alpha}^{*} = \frac{VaR_{\alpha}}{MtM_{P}}$$

where MtM_{P} is the portfolio MtM. We have

- Relative historical VaR:

$$VaR_{99\%}^{*} = \frac{\$4576.77}{\$88\,368.80} = 5.18\%$$

- Relative Gaussian VaR:

$$VaR_{99\%}^{*} = \frac{\$3190.79}{\$88\,368.80} = 3.61\%$$

THE GAUSSIAN ES

The Gaussian ES is straightforward to compute once you know the Gaussian VaR definition. The only change lies in the term before the portfolio volatility σ(P&L), that is the quantile. In the Gaussian VaR definition, the term Φ_α^{-1} denotes the inverse of the standardized Gaussian (or normal) distribution, and we call it the quantile. We have

$$\text{VaR}_\alpha^G = -\mu(\text{P\&L}) + \Phi_\alpha^{-1} \times \sigma(\text{P\&L})$$

In the Gaussian ES, the term before the portfolio volatility is not a quantile, and should be considered as a scaling factor instead. As shown in the circle below, this scaling factor is calculated from Φ_α^{-1}, but not only that. We have

$$\text{ES}_\alpha^G = -\mu(\text{P\&L}) + \left(\frac{\phi\left(\Phi_\alpha^{-1}\right)}{(1-\alpha)} \right) \times \sigma(\text{P\&L})$$

Scaling factor of Gaussian ES

where

- $\phi(x)$ is the probability density function (pdf) of the standardized Gaussian distribution.
- Φ_α^{-1} is the quantile of the standardized Gaussian distribution used to compute the Gaussian VaR ($\Phi(x)$ is the cdf of the standardized Gaussian distribution).

We can compute the scaling factor of the Gaussian ES with the statistical functions of Excel. Assuming a confidence level of 99%, we proceed in three steps (for each Excel function below, its arguments appear in bold):

- Step 1. Calculation of $\Phi_{99\%}^{-1}$
  Excel function: NORM.S.N(**0.99**)
  Output: 2.32634787
- Step 2. Calculation of $\phi\left(\Phi_{99\%}^{-1}\right)$
  Excel function: NORM.S.DIST(**2.32634787**; **WRONG**)
  Output: 0.02665214

■ Step 3. Calculation of the scaling factor:

$$\frac{\phi\left(\Phi_{99\%}^{-1}\right)}{(1-99\%)} = \frac{0.02665214}{0.01}$$

Output: 2.66521422

In **Table 10**, we report the quantile Φ_{α}^{-1} and the scaling factor used in the VaR and ES calculation for different confidence levels. As shown in the table, there is an equivalence between both. For example, we note that a 99% VaR (Basel II and 2.5 frameworks) corresponds to a 97.5% ES (Basel III). Therefore, calculating a 97.5% ES simply consists of replacing $\Phi_{99\%}^{-1} = 2.3263$ by the scaling factor for ES at the 97.5% confidence level: 2.3378. This is so simple because the only difference between VaR and ES is the difference between the quantile for VaR and the scaling factor for ES.

The Gaussian ES at the 97.5% level is thus

$$ES_{97.5\%}^{G} = \underbrace{-\mu\,(\text{P\&L})}_{\substack{\text{Same value as in} \\ \text{the VaR calculation}}} + \underbrace{2.3378 \times \sigma(\text{P\&L})}_{\substack{\text{Same value as in} \\ \text{the VaR calculation}}}$$

$$= -\$50.95 + 2.3378 \times \$1393.52$$

$$= \$3206.82$$

If we compare the Gaussian with the historical ES, we have

■ $ES_{97.5\%}^{H} = \$3925.37$
■ $ES_{97.5\%}^{G} = \$3206.82$

TABLE 10 Quantiles and scaling factors for different confidence levels α

α	99.99%	99.9%	99%	97.5%	95%	90%
Φ_{α}^{-1} for VaR	3.7190	3.0902	2.3263	1.9600	1.6449	1.2816
Scaling factor for ES	3.9585	3.36701	2.6652	2.3378	2.0627	1.7550

Again, we observe that the historical ES is higher than its Gaussian counterpart. What we noted for historical and Gaussian VaR holds true for ES. This is not surprising, because VaR and ES are related to each other. We can conclude from the above historical/Gaussian ES (97.5% confidence level) that the probability of our Google/Amazon portfolio experiencing an average loss of $3925.37/$3206.82 over the next 24 hours is 2.5%. In contrast, the historical/Gaussian VaR (99% confidence level) estimate of the probability of incurring a loss higher than $4576.77/$3190.85 over the next 24 hours is 1%.

NOTES

1. A closed-form expression (or closed-form solution) is any formula that can be expressed analytically in terms of a finite number of standard operations and "well-known" functions. When analytical solutions are too complex or are unavailable, numerical simulations are used. A closed-form solution is exact whereas a numerical solution is only approximate.
2. The Gaussian (or normal) and Student's t distributions are the two best known theoretical probability distributions.
3. Another interesting property of the covariance matrix is to be positive semidefinite (a symmetric matrix with non-negative eigenvalues).
4. Although closely related terms, there is a slight difference between both concepts. In a nutshell, the covariance tells us that two variables (e.g., two asset returns such as Google and Amazon) change in the same way, while correlation reveals the strength of the linear relationship between asset returns and how a change in one asset return affects a change in the other.
5. We have $\sigma_p = 2.9470\% = \sqrt{\sigma_p^2} = \sqrt{0.0868\%}$.
6. The terms "quantile" and "percentile" are often used interchangeably. This is not totally accurate, since percentiles are examples of quantiles.
7. In contrast to the mean calculation, different approaches are available for modelling the covariance between asset returns. We have used the empirical covariance matrix or the empirical standard deviation to estimate the P&L volatility of our Google/Amazon portfolio. Another approach widely used in risk management is to consider that the volatility is time-varying. This model is known as a GARCH(p, q) process or Generalized Autoregressive Conditional Heteroscedasticity.
8. The two statistical indicators of skewness and kurtosis will be addressed later in the book.

## CHAPTER 9

A Brief Overview of
Monte Carlo Simulation

Among many other potential applications, Monte Carlo simulation can be used to generate a collection of random market risk factor scenarios.[1] Considering our Google/Amazon portfolio, the market risk factor is defined as the return of each stock. Indeed, any decreases in daily stock prices will generate a negative return and thus a loss in value. This holds true for the Profit and Loss (P&L).

The general idea of Monte Carlo simulation is to generate market risk factors from a theoretical probability distribution (think about the Gaussian model) while preserving the correlation between asset returns in the portfolio. Ideally, the selected theoretical distribution should not be too far from the assets or portfolio observed/historical distributions. The "garbage in, garbage out" rule also applies here.

The Monte Carlo methodology consists of three major steps:

1. **Scenario generation.** Using the volatility and correlation estimates for the assets in the portfolio (Google and Amazon), we produce n simulations of market risk factors (returns) in accordance with a theoretical probability distribution (unsurprisingly, the Gaussian framework is the easiest to use).
2. **Portfolio valuation.** For each scenario, we compute a simulated value of the portfolio value.
3. **Risk measure.** We then compute a quantile for a given confidence level to compute the Value-at-Risk (VaR).

In conclusion, the Monte Carlo method is simply another way to simulate market risk factors (returns). Within the historical VaR framework, we used a different method to simulate data by shocking the current prices of Google and Amazon through historical returns observed over the last 250 trading days. The shocked returns obtained were then used to compute a simulated P&L. Therefore, Monte Carlo and historical VaRs are very close in terms of their underlying logic. Both are grounded on simulated risk factors.

The former uses risk factors simulated from a theoretical probability distribution, whereas the latter prefers historical/observed returns.

Figure 13 displays the frequency distribution of 100 000 simulated P&L values for the Google/Amazon portfolio, through a Gaussian distribution used as the theoretical probability distribution. We note that **Figure 13** is pretty much like the perfect bell-shaped Gaussian curve. This is not surprising. If the returns do not deviate too much from the Gaussian assumption and the number of simulations is high, the Monte Carlo VaR must be pretty close to the Gaussian VaR calculated previously.[2]

Using the quantile method,[3] we obtain a Monte Carlo VaR at the 99% confidence level $\left(\text{VaR}^{MC}_{99\%}\right)$ equal to \$3183.21, which is not so far from the Gaussian VaR $\left(\text{VaR}^{G}_{99\%}\right)$ equal to \$3190.85. It should be noted, however, that the Monte Carlo VaR results are highly sensitive to the number of simulations. As an example, with 10 000 simulations, we have $\text{VaR}^{MC}_{99\%} = \$3326.34$.

The Monte Carlo VaR is often considered as a panacea for VaR calculation – probably due to its apparent sophistication. This is a huge mistake. Never forget that the Monte Carlo VaR accuracy depends entirely on the fit between the observed distribution and the theoretical probability distribution used to generate returns and then P&L scenarios. Therefore, the Monte Carlo VaR is nothing more than an estimate, as the historical VaR is. Specifically, a twofold estimate since we first estimate the volatility and correlation parameters to generate scenarios, and then estimate a quantile to compute the VaR. In some sense, we can say that the Monte Carlo VaR we have

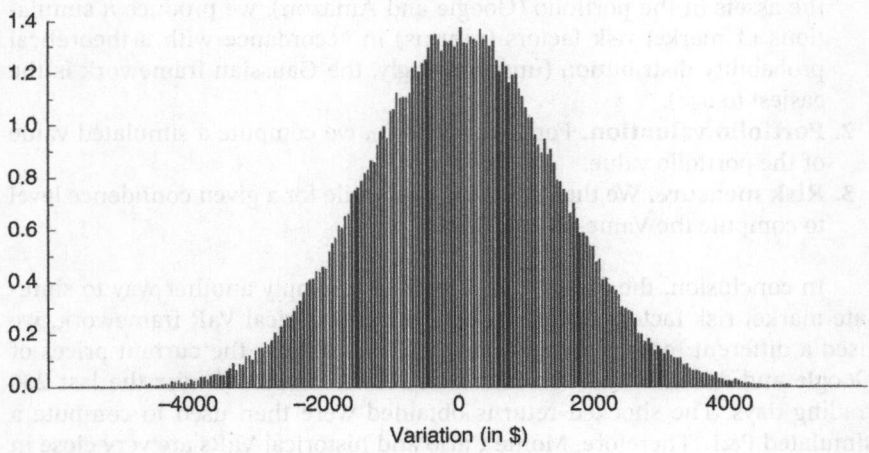

FIGURE 13 Frequency distribution of simulated P&L

calculated $\left(\text{VaR}_{99\%}^{MC} = \$3326.34\right)$ is a kind of hybrid between the Gaussian VaR (we estimate parameters) and the historical VaR (we estimate a quantile of the P&L distribution).[4]

When it comes to computing a Monte Carlo VaR, the theoretical probability distribution to be selected is critical. Bear in mind the "garbage in, garbage out" rule. In the field of finance, the Gaussian distribution is used extensively to model financial asset returns, due to its mathematical tractability (simulating a Gaussian vector is standard practice in finance). However, it is well known that the model risk is high when using the Gaussian distribution in risk management. To make a long story short, the Gaussian VaR underestimates the potential loss that could be incurred on a portfolio. This is obviously an acute problem for risk management.

The computational burden of Monte Carlo methods is not to be underestimated. Technically speaking, generating n independent variates (or random variables) such as, for example, financial asset returns and then combining these variates so as to achieve the desired correlations is not that easy. It requires using methods to decompose the covariance matrix. The most popular is the so-called Cholesky decomposition (or factorization). Without going into unnecessary technical details, it is worth mentioning that the Cholesky algorithm requires a positive-definite covariance matrix to provide a decomposition. With two assets in a portfolio this is not a problem, but with large matrices obtained from a financial institution dataset this property does not always hold true.

NOTES

1. For example, Monte Carlo methods are helpful to simulate credit rating dynamics of corporate firms over a specified time horizon in the future, or to compute integrals.
2. 100 000 may reasonably be considered as a very large number of simulations.
3. To compute the Monte Carlo VaR, we calculate the quantile of the 100 000 simulated P&L values at the specified confidence level (99%). We do not use the quantile of the standardized Gaussian distribution $\left(\Phi_{99\%}^{-1}\right)$ as we did previously. That is the difference between the Monte Carlo VaR (assuming Gaussian returns) and the theoretical Gaussian VaR calculated using the theoretical quantile Φ_α^{-1}.
4. As a reminder, the Gaussian VaR is a parametric VaR since it is grounded on the mean and standard deviation (volatility).

CHAPTER **10**

Risk Contribution

RISK DECOMPOSITION OF THE GAUSSIAN VaR

So far, we have computed two risk measures: Value-at-Risk (VaR) and Expected Shortfall (ES) in two different frameworks: Gaussian and historical. The next step from a risk management standpoint is to think in terms of risk contribution. The idea is to allocate risk efficiently within a portfolio of financial assets.

A risk measure gives an estimate of the global or total risk exposure of a portfolio. Thanks to previous VaR and ES calculations, we know the risk exposure of our Google/Amazon portfolio—expressed as a potential loss over the next 24 hours. Although useful, this information is not enough to identify the sources of risk. We need to disentangle the total risk of our portfolio to understand where it comes from: mainly Google, mainly Amazon or both? Simply put, we aim to identify the potential risk concentration within our portfolio. This notion of risk contribution echoes with the portfolio risk profile, and is at the core of risk allocation strategies. Remember the risk reduction generated through portfolio diversification.

The risk allocation principle consists of breaking down the portfolio total risk into a sum of risk contributions by sub-portfolios. The scope can be traders or asset managers, desks, asset classes or any other risk unit that makes sense in terms of risk exposure. This is a salient issue for financial institutions because risk allocation is linked to capital allocation, another important issue as it directly impacts the profitability of business units.

The risk contribution of the ith asset in a portfolio, RC_i, is defined as the product of the so-called marginal VaR by the exposure (or nominal) of this asset:

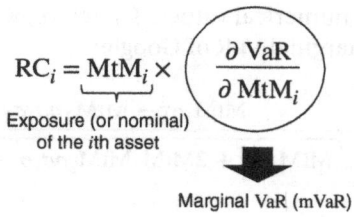

$$RC_i = \underbrace{MtM_i}_{\substack{\text{Exposure (or nominal)} \\ \text{of the } i\text{th asset}}} \times \left(\frac{\partial \, VaR}{\partial \, MtM_i} \right)$$

Marginal VaR (mVaR)

79

We can decompose our two-asset portfolio into two sub-portfolios and calculate the risk contribution of Google and Amazon to the portfolio total risk. The marginal VaR (mVaR) is a sensitivity measure of the VaR. It can be either positive or negative, and indicates how much the VaR will move when the exposure of the ith asset in a portfolio increases or decreases. The marginal VaR can thus be considered as the marginal risk of the ith asset.

Technically speaking, the marginal VaR is the first-order partial derivative of the VaR with respect to the exposure of the ith asset.[1] Where the marginal VaR is negative, the risk contribution is also negative. An asset whose risk contribution is negative is a portfolio risk diversifier, meaning that it has a significant impact in terms of risk reduction.

Interestingly, both VaR and ES satisfy Euler's principle.[2] Thanks to this allocation property, we can disentangle the portfolio total risk and isolate the portion of risk attributable to the ith asset. This means that the sum of the risk contributions is always equal to the portfolio VaR or ES. The risk contribution of the ith asset (or sub-portfolio) cannot be higher than the standalone risk measure (VaR or ES) due to risk diversification.

In order to compute the risk contributions of Google and Amazon, we recall that the nominal exposures are \$26 507.80 (Google) and \$61 861.00 (Amazon). The estimated volatility of daily returns is 1.5309% for Google and 1.8362% for Amazon. The correlation of stock returns is 52.8189% and the expected returns are \$31.20 (Google) and \$19.75 (Amazon). We know the Gaussian VaR of the Google/Amazon portfolio at the 99% confidence level for a 1-day holding period: $\text{VaR}_{99\%}^{G} = \$3190.85$. Calculating the risk contribution of the two assets in the portfolio means disentangling this amount of \$3190.85 to identify a potential risk concentration on Google or Amazon.

We start with the calculation of the marginal VaR of Google (we consider this as the first asset in the portfolio), defined as the first-order partial derivative of the portfolio VaR with respect to the exposure (or nominal) of the first asset in the portfolio (Google):

$$mVaR_1 = \frac{\partial VaR_P}{\partial MtM_1}$$

After calculation, we obtain the following expression for $mVaR_1$, for which we know all the numerical values. Therefore, we just have to copy and paste them to get the marginal VaR of Google:

$$mVaR_1 = -\mu_1 + \Phi_{99\%}^{-1} \frac{MtM_1\sigma_1^2 + MtM_2\rho\sigma_1\sigma_2}{\sqrt{MtM_1^2\sigma_1^2 + 2MtM_1MtM_2\rho\sigma_1\sigma_2 + MtM_2^2\sigma_2^2}} \blacktriangleright \begin{array}{l}\text{Portfolio}\\\text{volatility}\end{array}$$

where

- $\Phi_{99\%}^{-1}$ is the quantile (99% confidence level) of the standardized Gaussian distribution.
- MtM_1 and MtM_2 are the nominal exposures of Google and Amazon (as of 22 February 2022).
- σ_1 and σ_2 are the volatilities of Google and Amazon (σ_1^2 and σ_2^2 are their variances).
- ρ is the coefficient of correlation between the daily returns of Google and Amazon.

The $mVaR_1$ equation above is not as complicated as it appears. We know the end result of the denominator, since we calculated the portfolio volatility (expressed in value or, equivalently, in MtM terms) to compute the Gaussian VaR. It was equal to $1393.52. The marginal VaR of Google is thus[3]

$$mVaR_1 = -0.1177\% + 2.3263 \times \frac{15.40}{1393.52} = 0.0245$$

The risk contribution of Google is then

$$RC_1 = MtM_1 \times mVaR_1$$

$$= \$26\,507.80 \times 0.0245 = \$650.17$$

The marginal VaR of Amazon (the second asset in the portfolio) is defined as the first-order partial derivative of the portfolio VaR with respect to the exposure of the second asset in the portfolio (Amazon):

$$mVaR_2 = \frac{\partial VaR_P}{\partial MtM_2}$$

We deduce that

$$mVaR_2 = -\mu_2 + \Phi_{99\%}^{-1} \frac{MtM_2\sigma_2^2 + MtM_1\rho\sigma_1\sigma_2}{\sqrt{MtM_1^2\sigma_1^2 + 2MtM_1MtM_2\rho\sigma_1\sigma_2 + MtM_2^2\sigma_2^2}} \quad \blacktriangleright \begin{array}{l}\text{Portfolio}\\\text{volatility}\end{array}$$

$$= -0.0319\% + 2.3263 \times \frac{24.79}{1393.52} = 0.0411$$

The portfolio volatility in $mVaR_1$ and $mVaR_2$ is of course the same. This drastically simplifies the calculation of the marginal VaR. The risk contribution of Amazon is then

$$RC_2 = MtM_2 \times mVaR_2$$

$$= \$61\,861 \times 0.0411 = \$2540.68$$

We can easily check the accuracy of our results as we know that the sum of the two risk contributions must be equal to the portfolio Gaussian VaR at the 99% confidence level:

$$\underbrace{RC_1}_{} + \underbrace{RC_2}_{} = \$650.17 + \$2540.66 = \underbrace{\$3190.85 = VaR_{99\%}^{G}}_{}$$

Google risk   Amazon risk   Portfolio Gaussian VaR
contribution   contribution

In order to clarify the profile of our Google/Amazon portfolio, we report in **Table 11** the risk contributions of both assets.

In **Table 11**, MtM_i denotes the exposure (or nominal) of the first asset ($i = 1$: Google) and the second asset ($i = 2$: Amazon) in the portfolio. $RC_i^{\%}$ stands for the risk decomposition of Google and Amazon expressed as a percentage, calculated as follows:

$$RC_i^{\%} = \frac{RC_i}{VaR_{99\%}^{G}}$$

We check that

$$RC_1^{\%} + RC_2^{\%} = 100\%$$

We have previously calculated the weights of Google and Amazon in the portfolio: $w_G = 30\%$ and $w_A = 70\%$. We can thus conclude that Amazon explains almost 80% of the portfolio risk, whereas it represents 70% of the portfolio allocation. Clearly, Amazon is the main risk driver of this portfolio. That said, this cannot be a surprise given the large difference between the weight of each asset in the portfolio: 30% for Google against 70% for Amazon.

TABLE 11   Risk decomposition of the Gaussian VaR

Asset	MtM_i	$mVaR_i$	RC_i	$RC_i^{\%}$
Google	\$26 507.80	0.0245	\$650.17	20.38%
Amazon	\$61 861.00	0.0411	\$2540.68	79.62%
$VaR_{99\%}^{G}$			\$3190.85	

To put it differently, Amazon accounts for 70% of the total portfolio exposure, and explains about 80% of its risk.

Although Google and Amazon operate in different industries, it is worth noting that the correlation between asset returns is high: 52.82%, meaning we cannot expect a significant diversification gain (risk reduction). Due to both the concentration of risk on Amazon and the low diversification gain expected, the risk profile of this portfolio may not be considered balanced. Depending on his/her risk aversion, an investor might reduce the Amazon exposure.

RISK DECOMPOSITION OF THE GAUSSIAN ES

The risk decomposition of the Gaussian ES follows the same logic as for the Gaussian VaR. We have calculated the Gaussian ES at the 97.5% confidence level: $3206.82. The sum of Google and Amazon risk contributions must be equal to the portfolio risk measured with the ES.

As a reminder, the Gaussian VaR and ES only differ in the constant term: the quantile of the standardized normal distribution Φ_α^{-1} for the VaR and the scaling factor $\phi(\Phi_\alpha^{-1})/(1-\alpha)$ for the ES. The calculation of the marginal ES, denoted mES_i, simplifies to the calculation of the scaling factor. To compute mES_i, we just have to copy and paste the values computed to get the marginal Gaussian VaR, and replace Φ_α^{-1} by the scaling factor of the Gaussian ES. For Google:

$$mES_1 = \underbrace{-\mu_1 +}_{\substack{\text{Same as for} \\ \text{mVaR}_1}} \frac{\phi(\Phi_{99\%}^{-1})}{(1-99\%)} \times \underbrace{\frac{MtM_1\sigma_1^2 + MtM_2\rho\sigma_1\sigma_2}{\sqrt{MtM_1^2\sigma_1^2 + 2MtM_1MtM_2\rho\sigma_1\sigma_2 + MtM_2^2\sigma_2^2}}}_{\substack{\text{Same as for the marginal Gaussian VaR: } mVaR_1}} \leftarrow \text{Portfolio volatility}$$

$$= -0.1177\% + 2.3378 \times \frac{15.40}{1393.52} = 0.0247$$

The risk contribution of Google is then

$$RC_1 = MtM_1 \times mES_1$$

$$= \$26\,507.80 \times 0.0247 = \$653.53$$

TABLE 12   Risk decomposition of the 99% Gaussian ES

Asset	MtM$_i$	mES$_i$	RC$_i$	RC$_i^\%$
Google	\$26 507.80	0.0247	\$653.53	20.38%
Amazon	\$61 861.00	0.047113	\$2553.29	79.62%
ES$_{99\%}^G$			\$3206.82	

The marginal VaR of Amazon is as follows:

$$mES_2 = -\mu_2 + \underbrace{\frac{\phi\left(\Phi_{99\%}^{-1}\right)}{(1-99\%)}}_{\substack{\text{Same as for} \\ \text{mVaR}_2}} \times \underbrace{\frac{MtM_2\sigma_2^2 + MtM_1\rho\sigma_1\sigma_2}{\sqrt{MtM_1^2\sigma_1^2 + 2MtM_1MtM_2\rho\sigma_1\sigma_2 + MtM_2^2\sigma_2^2}}}_{\substack{\text{Same as for the marginal Gaussian VaR: mVaR}_2}} \blacktriangleright \begin{array}{l}\text{Portfolio}\\\text{volatility}\end{array}$$

$$= -0.0319\% + 2.3378 \times \frac{15.40}{1393.52} = 0.0413$$

The risk contribution of Amazon is then

$$RC_2 = MtM_2 \times mES_2$$
$$= \$61\,861 \times 0.0413 = \$2553.29$$

The results are summarized in **Table 12**.

Unsurprisingly, the risk profile of the Google/Amazon portfolio is not altered when we use the 97.5% ES instead of the 99% VaR. The results displayed in **Tables 11 and 12** are very similar to each other because the 99% VaR is close to the 97.5% ES:

- $VaR_{99\%}^G = \$3190.85$
- $ES_{97.5\%}^G = \$3206.82$

RISK DECOMPOSITION OF THE HISTORICAL VaR

The risk decomposition of the historical VaR follows the same logic as the Gaussian VaR, but the calculation of the risk contribution of both assets in the portfolio is based on the order statistics.

TABLE 13 Duplication of Table 8 (The six worst P&L scenarios)

#	Date	P&L ($) ↑	Order statistic
11	2022-02-03	-5712.47	$P\&L_{1:250}$
145	2021-07-30	-4884.90	$P\&L_{2:250}$
20	2022-01-21	-4268.64	$P\&L_{3:250}$
5	2022-02-11	-3050.94	$P\&L_{4:250}$
241	2021-03-18	-2900.51	$P\&L_{5:250}$
18	2022-01-25	-2734.77	$P\&L_{6:250}$

We found that the 99% historical VaR of the Google/Amazon portfolio, $\text{VaR}_{99\%}^{H}$, was \$4576.77. The sum of the risk contributions must still be $\text{VaR}_{99\%}^{H} = \$4576.77$. We obtained $\text{VaR}_{99\%}^{H}$ through a linear interpolation[4] between the second and third worst Profit and Loss (P&L) occurrences, that is the second- and third-order statistics of the portfolio P&L distribution: $P\&L_{2:250} = -\$4884.90$ and $P\&L_{3:250} = -\$4268.64$. For the sake of clarity, we reproduce **Table 8** here as **Table 13**, which displays the six worst P&L outcomes.

To compute the risk contributions, we first identify the rank of the second and third-order statistics. The rank is identified by the symbol # in **Table 13**. The rank of the second- and third-order statistics $P\&L_{2:250} = -\$4884.90$ and $P\&L_{3:250} = -\$4268.64$ is #145 and #20, respectively. In other words, the second- and third-order statistics correspond to the 20th and 145th historical scenarios. Similarly, the first- and fifth-order statistics in **Table 13** correspond to the 11th and 241st historical scenarios.

Then, we search for the simulated (or shocked) prices of Google and Amazon corresponding to the ranks #145 and #20. **Table 14** is an extract of the whole distribution of Google and Amazon shocked prices.

As shown in **Table 14**, the shocked price of Google corresponding to rank #20 is \$2592.00, and \$2630.26 for rank #145. For Amazon, the shocked prices are \$2909.01 and \$2859.06 for ranks #20 and #145, respectively. We calculate the risk contribution of Google ($i = 1$) and Amazon ($i = 2$) as follows:

$$\text{RC}_i = -\underbrace{(n \times (1 - \alpha) - n^*)}_{\substack{= 250 \times (1 - 99\%) - 2 \\ = 2.5 - 2 \\ = 0.5}} \times \underbrace{(P\&L_{i,\#20} + P\&L_{i,\#145})}_{\substack{\text{P\&L} = \underbrace{\text{Simulated value}}_{\substack{\text{Number of stocks} \\ \times \\ \text{Shocked stock price}}} - \underbrace{\text{Current value}}_{\substack{\text{Number of stocks} \\ \times \\ \text{Current stock price} \\ (2022\text{-}02\text{-}17)}}}}$$

where

- $n^* = 2$ is the inferior integer part of $n \times (1 - 99\%) = 2.5$.
- $P\&L_{i,\#20}$ is the P&L of the ith asset in the portfolio, calculated from the 20th shocked price and the current price.

TABLE 14　Distribution of Google and Amazon shocked prices (extract)

| # | Date | Shocked prices | |
		$P_{s,G}$ ($)	$P_{s,A}$ ($)
1	2022-02-17	2550.72	3025.59
2	2022-02-16	2672.70	3124.47
3	2022-02-15	2671.95	3119.83
...	...	...	...
19	2022-01-24	2659.98	3134.27
20	2022-01-21	2592.00	2909.01
21	2022-01-20	2615.29	3001.40
...	...	...	...
144	2021-08-02	2653.30	3096.67
145	2021-07-30	2630.26	2859.06
146	2021-07-29	2644.62	3067.15
...	...	...	...
249	2021-03-08	2537.56	3043.04
250	2021-03-05	2733.07	3116.83
251	2021-03-04	NA	NA

Note: $P_{s,G}$ ($) and $P_{s,A}$ ($) denote the respective shocked (or simulated) prices of Google and Amazon.

- $\text{P\&L}_{i,\#145} = 10 \times (\$2630.26 - \$2650.78)$ is the P&L of the ith asset in the portfolio, calculated from the 145th shocked price and the current price.

With 10 Google and 20 Amazon stocks in the portfolio, it follows that

$$\text{RC}_1 = -\left(\underbrace{-205.20}_{\text{P\&L}_{1,\#145}} + \left(0.5 \times \left(\underbrace{-587.80}_{} + 205.20\right)\right)\right)$$

$$\underbrace{10 \times (\$2630.26 - \$2650.78)}_{} \quad \underbrace{10 \times (\$2592.0 - \$2650.78)}_{\text{P\&L}_{1,\#20}}$$

$$\text{RC}_1 = \$396.50$$

For Amazon:

$$\text{RC}_2 = -\left(\underbrace{-4679.80}_{\text{P\&L}_{2,\#145}} + \left(0.5 \times \left(\underbrace{-3680.80}_{} + 4679.80\right)\right)\right)$$

$$\underbrace{20 \times (\$2589.05 - \$3093.05)}_{} \quad \underbrace{20 \times (\$2909.01 - \$3093.05)}_{\text{P\&L}_{2,\#20}}$$

$$\text{RC}_2 = \$4180.30$$

We check that

$$RC_1 + RC_2 = \$396.5 + \$4180.3 = \$4576.8 = VaR_{99\%}^H$$

The exact value of $VaR_{99\%}^H$ is \$4576.77.

To compute the marginal risk of the ith asset in the portfolio, $mVaR_i$, we no longer use the Mark-to-Market (MtM_i, in \$) as with the Gaussian VaR risk contribution, but the weight of each asset expressed as a percentage. As a reminder, we have $w_G = 30.0\%$ and $w_A = 70.0\%$, and the risk contribution is thus defined as follows:

$$RC_i = \underbrace{w_i}_{\substack{\text{Weight of the }i\text{th}\\\text{asset (in \%)}}} \times \underbrace{mVaR_i}_{\substack{\text{Marginal VaR}}}$$

The marginal risks of Google and Amazon are then

$$mVaR_1 = \frac{396.50}{30\%} = 1321.70$$

$$mVaR_2 = \frac{4180.30}{70\%} = 5971.86$$

We summarize the results in **Table 15**.

We note that the risk decomposition is modified depending on the risk measure used. With the historical VaR, the portfolio risk is even more concentrated on Amazon, since its risk contribution represents 91.33% against only 79.62% with the Gaussian VaR. The explanation is purely technical. Because the risk contribution is based on two parameters (which is very few)—the exposure (\$) or the weight (%) and the marginal risk—its computation is

TABLE 15 Risk decomposition of the 99% historical VaR

Asset	w_i	$mVaR_i$	RC_i	$RC_i^\%$
Google	30.0%	1321.70	\$396.50	8.66%
Amazon	70.0%	5971.86	\$4180.30	91.33%
$VaR_{99\%}^H$			\$4576.80	

highly sensitive to the risk measure itself. We have seen that the Gaussian and historical VaR are drastically different per se.

RISK DECOMPOSITION OF THE HISTORICAL ES

We recall that the historical ES is calculated by averaging the $n \times (1-\alpha)$ first-order statistics of the P&L, that is the P&L values larger than or equal to the VaR. When $n = 250$ and $\alpha = 97.5\%$, as required under Basel III, the product $n \times (1-\alpha)$ is not an integer (we obtain 6.25) and we use $n*$, the inferior integer part of 6.25, that is 6. As a result, the 97.5% historical ES corresponds to the average of the six worst P&L occurrences. Following this line, we found $\mathrm{ES}^{\mathrm{H}}_{97.5\%} = \$3925.37$.

To provide the reader with a clear vision of what happens with the computation of the 97.5% historical ES, because it is useful for understanding the ES risk contribution, we reproduce in **Table 16** the seven worst P&L values. The 97.5% historical VaR is also reported.

As shown in **Table 16**, there are six P&L occurrences greater than or equal to $\mathrm{VaR}^{\mathrm{H}}_{97.5\%}$ and only two greater than or equal to $\mathrm{VaR}^{\mathrm{H}}_{99\%}$. Therefore, to obtain $\mathrm{ES}^{\mathrm{H}}_{99\%} = -\$5298.69$, we average the two P&L values greater than or equal to $\mathrm{VaR}^{\mathrm{H}}_{99\%} = -\$4576.77$. To obtain $\mathrm{ES}^{\mathrm{H}}_{97.5\%} = -\$3925.37$, we average the six P&L values greater than or equal to $\mathrm{VaR}^{\mathrm{H}}_{97.5\%} = -\$2705.27$.

For the risk contribution of Google and Amazon with the historical ES at the 99% confidence level, the sequential steps are exactly the same as for the risk contribution with the 99% historical VaR.

We start by counting how many order statistics are greater than or equal to $\mathrm{VaR}^{\mathrm{H}}_{99\%}$. **Table 16** indicates that only the first- and second-order statistics $\mathrm{P\&L}_{1:250}$ and $\mathrm{P\&L}_{2:250}$ are greater than or equal to $\mathrm{VaR}^{\mathrm{H}}_{99\%} = -\$4576.77$. Then,

TABLE 16 Historical VaR and ES

#	Date	P&L ($)	Order statistic	
11	2022-02-03	-5712.47	$\mathrm{P\&L}_{1:250}$	$ES^H_{99\%}$ (rows 1–2); $ES^H_{97.5\%}$ (rows 1–6)
145	2021-07-30	-4884.90	$\mathrm{P\&L}_{2:250}$	
20	2022-01-21	-4268.64	$\mathrm{P\&L}_{3:250}$	$\leftarrow VaR^H_{99\%} = -\$4576.77$
5	2022-02-11	-3050.94	$\mathrm{P\&L}_{4:250}$	
241	2021-03-18	-2900.51	$\mathrm{P\&L}_{5:250}$	
18	2022-01-25	-2734.77	$\mathrm{P\&L}_{6:250}$	
108	2021-09-28	-2616.79	$\mathrm{P\&L}_{7:250}$	$\leftarrow VaR^H_{97.5\%} = -\$2705.27$

we identify the rank of these two order statistics. From **Table 16**, where the symbol # defines rank, we have

- Rank of the first-order statistic $\text{P\&L}_{1:250} = -\$5712.47 \rightarrow \#11$
- Rank of the second-order statistic $\text{P\&L}_{2:250} = -\$4884.90 \rightarrow \#145$

The first- and second-order statistics correspond to the 11th and 145th historical scenarios.

Then, we search for the simulated (or shocked) prices of Google and Amazon corresponding to ranks #11 and #145. From **Table 17**, we have

- Shocked price of Google corresponding to rank #11: $P_{s,G}(\#11) = \$2562.84$
- Shocked price of Amazon corresponding to rank #11: $P_{s,A}(\#11) = \$2851.40$
- Shocked price of Google corresponding to rank #145: $P_{s,G}(\#145) = \$2630.26$
- Shocked price of Amazon corresponding to rank #145: $P_{s,A}(\#145) = \$2859.06$

Finally, we compute the risk contributions as follows:

$$\text{RC}_i = -\frac{1}{n*} \times (\text{P\&L}_{i,\#11} + \text{P\&L}_{i,\#145})$$

TABLE 17 Distribution of Google and Amazon shocked prices (extract)

| # | Date | Shocked prices | |
		$P_{s,G}$ (\$)	$P_{s,A}$ (\$)
1	2022-02-17	2550.72	3025.59
...	...	...	...
10	2022-02-04	2654.54	3511.72
⑪	2022-02-03	2562.84	2851.40
12	2022-02-02	2850.22	3081,16
...	...	...	...
144	2021-08-02	2653.30	3096.67
⑭⑤	2021-07-30	2630.26	2859.06
146	2021-07-29	2644.62	3067.15
...	...	...	...

where n^* is the inferior integer part of $n \times (1-\alpha) = 250 \times (1-99\%) = 2.5$. We thus have $n^* = 2$.

For Google, it follows that

$$RC_1 = -\frac{1}{2} \times \underbrace{\left(10 \times (\$2562.84 - \$2650.78)\right)}_{\substack{P_{s,G} \text{ (#11) in \textbf{Table 17} – Current price} \\ \text{(2022-02-17)}}}^{\text{P\&L}_{1,\#11}} + \underbrace{\left(10 \times (\$2630.26 - \$2650.78)\right)}_{\substack{P_{s,G} \text{ (#145) in \textbf{Table 17} – Current price} \\ \text{(2022-02-17)}}}^{\text{P\&L}_{1,\#145}}$$

$$RC_1 = \$542.30$$

For Amazon:

$$RC_2 = -\frac{1}{2} \times \underbrace{\left(20 \times (\$2851.40 - \$3093.05)\right)}_{\substack{P_{s,A} \text{ (#11) in \textbf{Table 17} – Current price} \\ \text{(2022-02-17)}}}^{\text{P\&L}_{2,\#11}} + \underbrace{\left(20 \times (\$2859.06 - \$3093.05)\right)}_{\substack{P_{s,A} \text{ (#145) in \textbf{Table 17} – Current price} \\ \text{(2022-02-17)}}}^{\text{P\&L}_{2,\#145}}$$

$$RC_2 = \$4756.40$$

We check that

$$RC_1 + RC_2 = \$542.30 + \$4756.40 = \$5298.70 = ES_{99\%}^{H}$$

The exact value of $ES_{99\%}^{H}$ is \$5298.69. With the historical approach, we recall that the risk contribution of the ith asset in the portfolio is defined as

$$RC_i = \underbrace{w_i}_{\substack{\text{Weight of the } i\text{th} \\ \text{asset (in \%)}}} \times \underbrace{mES_i}_{\text{Marginal ES}}$$

Therefore, the marginal risk of Google and Amazon is, respectively

$$mES_1 = \frac{542.30}{30\%} = 1807.7$$

$$mES_2 = \frac{4756.40}{70\%} = 6794.86$$

TABLE 18   Risk decomposition of the 99% historical ES

Asset	w_i	mES_i	RC_i	$RC_i^\%$
Google	30.0%	1807.70	$542.30	10.23%
Amazon	70.0%	6794.86	$4756.40	89.77%
$ES_{99\%}^H$			$5298.70	

We summarize the results in **Table 18**.

For the risk decomposition of the 97.5% historical ES, we average the P&L occurrences greater than or equal to $VaR_{97.5\%}^H = -\$2705.27$ in **Table 16**. There are six P&L values corresponding to the first six order statistics: $P\&L_{1:250}, \cdots, P\&L_{6:250}$. With a 97.5% confidence level, we have

$$n \times (1 - \alpha) = 250 \times (1 - 97.5\%) = 6.25, \text{ and thus } n^* = 6$$

It follows that the risk contribution of Google is

$$RC_1 = -\frac{1}{6} \times (P\&L_{1,\#11} + P\&L_{1,\#145} + P\&L_{1,\#20} + P\&L_{1,\#5} + P\&L_{1,\#241} + P\&L_{1,\#18})$$

We obtain

$$RC_1 = \$677.14$$

For Amazon:

$$RC_2 = -\frac{1}{6} \times (P\&L_{2,\#11} + P\&L_{2,\#145} + P\&L_{2,\#20} + P\&L_{2,\#5} + P\&L_{2,\#241} + P\&L_{2,\#18})$$

We obtain

$$RC_2 = \$3248.22$$

The results are summarized in **Table 19**.

TABLE 19   Risk decomposition of the 97.5% historical ES

Asset	w_i	mES_i	RC_i	$RC_i^\%$
Google	30.0%	2257.13	$677.14	17.25%
Amazon	70.0%	4640.31	$3248.22	82.75%
$ES_{97.5\%}^H$			$3925.37	

NOTES

1. The ∂ symbol indicates partial derivative.
2. This desirable property of the full allocation principle is due to the Swiss mathematician Leonhard Euler. It indicates that all the total risk capital (no more, no less) is allocated to the individual sub-portfolios.
3. For the sake of clarity, we display the parameters in $mVaR_1$ rounded to four decimal places, but we use their exact values to compute $RC_1 = 650.14$. Using the rounded parameters returns 649.44 instead.
4. Because $n \times (1 - \alpha) = 250 \times (1 - 99\%) = 2.5$ is not an integer, see Step 5 in Chapter 7.

## CHAPTER 11

Shortcomings of Risk Metrics

THE PROBLEM OF STATIONARITY

To compute a Value-at-Risk (VaR) and thus an Expected Shortfall (ES)—since both are interrelated—over a given holding period or time horizon (e.g., the next 24 hours or 10 days), a very demanding assumption is required. This assumption is called stationarity.

We recall that VaR is nothing more than a quantile (theoretical or empirical) of a portfolio Profit and Loss (P&L) calculated for a specified confidence level α. With this aim, we use historical data to estimate the potential changes in value of this portfolio in the near future—the next 24 hours according to the Basel III regulatory framework.

Unfortunately, we do not know the future and thus what could occur in financial markets over the next 24 hours. As a result, to deliver a VaR figure, we must assume the stationarity of the portfolio change in value over the holding period. In other words, we consider that the near future will behave like the past. If so, it makes sense to derive a 24-hour VaR estimate from what happened over the past trading year in terms of P&L fluctuations.

Of course, such an assumption is unrealistic knowing what may occur in financial markets in just 5 minutes. However, without this stationarity assumption, the VaR calculation is not possible, simply because the best ever forecast model is unable to predict the future. Therefore, there is no other choice than to compute statistical parameters (e.g., the mean and standard deviation if we are interested in a Gaussian VaR) from historical or empirical data (what we know), and to consider those parameters as acceptable estimates of the same unknown parameters over the next 24 hours (what we need). **Figure 14** summarizes the stationarity assumption.

VOLATILITY MODELLING

In the Gaussian framework, we saw that the main issue is the covariance matrix calculation. As a reminder, this matrix includes both the variances (along the diagonal) and covariances (on both sides of the diagonal) of asset returns.

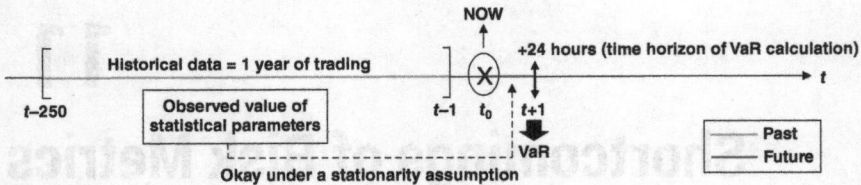

FIGURE 14   The stationarity assumption

Going back to our Google/Amazon portfolio, the risk factors are the stock prices of these two stocks. Indeed, any decrease in stock prices will generate a negative return, meaning a loss in value of the portfolio. The more or less drastic change in stock price volatility over a short time period may explain the magnitude of the loss. This is why volatility modelling and forecasting is an important tool in risk management.

To estimate the covariance matrix of asset returns/risk factors (recall that a return is calculated from two consecutive prices), we used the empirical variances of asset returns and the empirical covariances between asset returns. Then, we added the $(m \times m)$ elements up to estimate the empirical/historical standard deviation or volatility in order to get the Gaussian VaR. To illustrate, let's take a four-asset portfolio. Its covariance matrix Σ (or VCM) is defined as follows:

$$
\Sigma = \begin{pmatrix}
\sigma_1^2 & & & \\
\sigma_{21} & \sigma_2^2 & & \\
\sigma_{31} & \sigma_{32} & \sigma_3^2 & \\
\sigma_{41} & \sigma_{42} & \sigma_{43} & \sigma_4^2
\end{pmatrix}
$$

Variances of asset returns

Covariances between asset returns

For the sake of clarity, we do not reproduce the covariances in the upper-right triangle (above the diagonal) since they are exactly equal to those in the lower-left triangle (below the diagonal).

In the above covariance matrix, the variances and covariances for a given set of T returns are generally estimated as follows:

$$
\begin{cases}
\sigma_{R,t}^2 = \dfrac{1}{T}\sum_{j=1}^{T}(R_{t-j}-\bar{R})^2 & \blacktriangleright \text{ Variances of asset returns} \\[4mm]
\sigma_{12,t} = \dfrac{1}{T}\sum_{j=1}^{T}(R_{1,t-j}-\bar{R}_1)(R_{2,t-j}-\bar{R}_2) & \blacktriangleright \text{ Covariances between asset returns}
\end{cases}
$$

The issue with these statistical formulae is to produce equally weighted averages, meaning that each observation from $t-1$ to $t-T$ receives an equal weight in computing the variances and covariances. This implies that the losses incurred 6 months ago and yesterday will be equally important in the estimated variances and covariances (volatilities and correlations).[1]

In terms of risk exposure, this is wrong since the most recent losses are probably more impactful on the portfolio value than those realized several months ago. In financial markets, the most recent information is often the most relevant. Talking about volatility as an input for measuring risk with VaR, it might be more accurate to customize the variances and covariances formulae above in such a way that the weight of each historical data point decreases the further back we go in time.

The original method developed by RiskMetrics™ (1996) uses the Exponentially Weighted Moving Average (EWMA) model to forecast variances and covariances. The idea is to apply weights to a set of observations or data points with the weights declining exponentially over time. This results in weighting recent data more than data in the distant past. The variance and covariance equations become

$$0 < \lambda < 1 \begin{cases} \sigma_{R,t}^2 = (1-\lambda) \sum_{j=1}^{T} \lambda^{j-1} (R_{t-j} - \bar{R})^2 \quad \blacktriangleright \text{ Variances of asset returns} \\ \\ \sigma_{12,t} = (1-\lambda) \sum_{j=1}^{T} \lambda^{j-1} (R_{1,t-j} - \bar{R}_1)(R_{2,t-j} - \bar{R}_2) \quad \blacktriangleright \text{ Covariances between asset returns} \end{cases}$$

The parameter lambda (λ) is often referred to as the decay factor and denotes the weight applied in the exponential moving average. Its value is always bounded between zero and one and depends on the frequency of data. Lambda is 0.94 in the calculation of volatilities and correlations for a 1-day horizon and 0.97 for a 1-month horizon. The main advantage of this approach is that volatility reacts faster to shocks (large returns) as recent data carry more weight than data in the distant past.[2]

THE GAUSSIAN ASSUMPTION IS SEDUCTIVE BUT DANGEROUS

We mentioned that the Gaussian VaR has been criticized extensively due to its inability to take fat tails and skew effects into account. This leads to an underestimated VaR for two reasons:

- The fat tails phenomenon indicates that extreme price movements occur more frequently than implied by a normal distribution.
- A left or negatively skewed distribution means that unfavourable return outcomes occur more frequently than implied by a normal distribution.

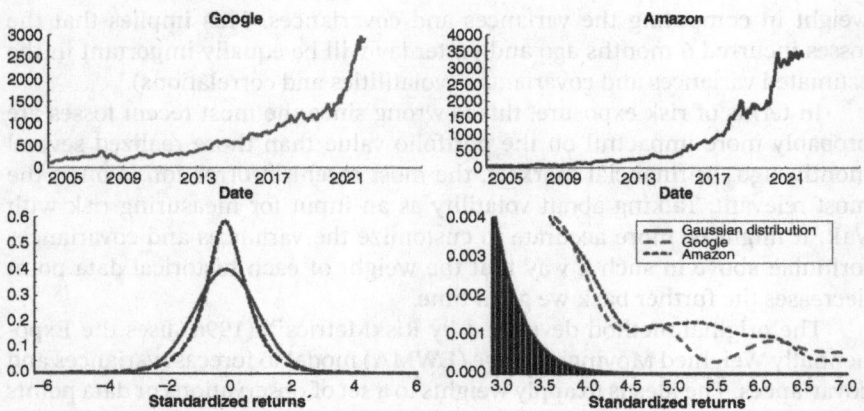

FIGURE 15   Focus on the tails of Google and Amazon

From a risk management perspective, underestimating risk is of course dangerous, since an expected loss may drastically impact the profitability of a bank, and further its resilience. While appealing due to its mathematical tractability, the Gaussian VaR may be dangerous because it depends only on the first two moments of the P&L distribution—the mean and the standard deviation.

By essence, the Gaussian VaR is thus unable to tell what happens in the tails, precisely where lies the truly dangerous risk for the bank. The graph in **Figure 15** shows what happens in the tails of Google and Amazon over the 2005–2022 time period with daily data (bottom right). We used the standardized returns $\dot{r}(t)$ of Google and Amazon, calculated as follows:

$$\dot{r}(t) = \frac{r(t) - \mu}{\sigma}$$

where $r(t)$ denotes the daily logarithmic returns of Google and Amazon; μ and σ are the mean and standard deviation of $r(t)$.[3]

The bottom-left graph displays three curves, even if only two are readily distinguishable. We first plot the density (or probability density function, pdf) of Google and Amazon standardized returns, $\dot{r}(t)$. These two distributions are built from the historical/observed returns. In other words, they are empirical distributions. They both peak at 0.6 on the y-axis. The third curve plotted below (0.4 on the y-axis) represents the Gaussian density. This is a theoretical distribution since it is built from a theoretical probability distribution. If the distributions of Google and Amazon standardized returns were actually Gaussian, that is $\dot{r}(t) \sim \mathcal{N}(0,1)$, they would match with the Gaussian density. This is not the case, since the peak of Google and Amazon distributions is higher than the Gaussian. This is a first indication of excess kurtosis, or higher kurtosis than the Gaussian distribution.

However, looking at the bottom-left graph, it is impossible to see what happens in the tails. This is due to the high number of data points used to build the three densities. The bottom-right graph in **Figure 15** zooms in on the tails of these three densities. As observed, the tails of Google and Amazon behave differently (erratically) from the Gaussian distribution (steadily decreasing) and exhibit significant fat tails. From a risk management viewpoint, such a pattern is obviously an acute problem since it means that extreme events are more probable than anticipated by the normal distribution.

From a statistical viewpoint, an extreme event (e.g., a financial crisis) is defined as a variation of plus or minus five standard deviations from the mean. Theoretically speaking, such an event should rarely occur since it is far from what happens on a regular basis or on average. It is thus located in the tail of a distribution, far from the mean. Unfortunately, there is a huge gap between what could occur theoretically speaking and the reality of financial markets. As an example, the Dow Jones lost 22.6% on 19 October 1987. This clearly indicates an extreme event related to the stock market crash. The theoretical probability of occurrence of such an event is estimated at $\frac{1}{10^{50}}$ (almost impossible). How many financial crises have there been since then?

It is also well known that most financial assets are significantly negatively skewed, meaning that return distributions are often tilted to the left (in the loss area). In short, when using the Gaussian VaR, you not only underestimate tail events (the occurrence of large losses because the VaR does not take gains into its calculation), but also the probability of incurring a few large losses (and frequent small gains) due to asymmetry of return distributions.

Two additional measures, known as kurtosis and skewness, characterize the relative peakedness or flatness (kurtosis) and the degree of asymmetry (skewness) of a given distribution compared to a Gaussian distribution and its bell-shaped curve. The kurtosis coefficient K is defined as

$$K = \frac{\mathbb{E}\left[\left(r_i - \mu\right)^4\right]}{\sigma^4}$$

where

$\mathbb{E}\,[\,] =$ mathematical expectation

r_i = returns on asset i

μ = average return on asset i

σ^4 = variance of returns squared

Since the Gaussian distribution has a kurtosis of 3 (mesokurtic), excess kurtosis is defined as $K - 3$ and denoted eK. When the excess kurtosis eK is strictly higher than zero, there are more occurrences far away from the mean than predicted by a standardized Gaussian (or normal) distribution. The asset returns distribution thus presents heavy tails and is said to be leptokurtic. When excess kurtosis is negative, the distribution has fewer extreme events than a normal distribution and is platykurtic (see Figure 16, bottom right).

Skewness characterizes the asymmetry of a distribution around its mean. The skewness coefficient is given by

$$S = \frac{\mathbb{E}\left[\left(r_i - \mu\right)^3\right]}{\sigma^3}$$

where σ^3 is the cube of volatility.

For the Gaussian distribution, skewness is zero (the Gaussian distribution is perfectly symmetric). Positive skewness indicates an asymmetric tail extending towards positive values (right-skewed). A right-skewed distribution is longer on the right side of its peak. Negative skewness implies asymmetry towards negative values (left-skewed). A left-skewed distribution is longer on the left side of its peak. Practitioners frequently work with the kurtosis and skewness coefficients defined above because they are more convenient than the kurtosis and skewness.[4] **Figure 16** illustrates the coefficients of kurtosis and skewness against the Gaussian distribution (the perfect bell-shaped curve) used as a benchmark. Positive and negative S on the plot indicate right and left-skewed distributions, respectively.

Having defined the kurtosis and skewness coefficients, one wonders whether it would not be easier to consider alternative probability distributions than the Gaussian. For example, the Student's t fat-tailed distribution or,

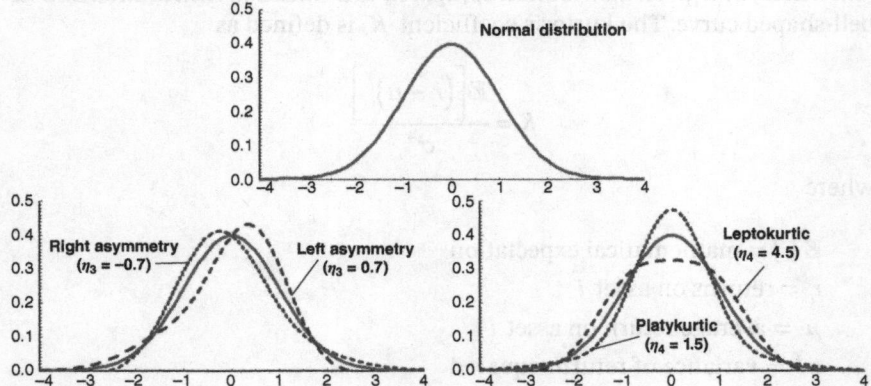

FIGURE 16   Skewness and kurtosis

even better, a skewed Student's t distribution to take asymmetry of financial asset returns into account. Another option could be Extreme Value Theory (EVT)-based models, which are dedicated to tail risk and rare events (a severe loss may occur with a very low probability). As mentioned by Thierry Roncalli, Head of Quantitative Research at Amundi Asset Management, several alternative probability distributions and methods are available, but most of them are not used in practice simply because they are not appealing from a professional standpoint.

TAMING FAT TAILS AND SKEWNESS

A possible solution to alleviate the drawbacks of the Gaussian VaR is to use the Cornish–Fisher method, which considers skewness and kurtosis. Interestingly, this alternative approach to calculate VaR is very popular among risk practitioners. The idea is to modify the quantile of the standardized normal distribution Φ_α^{-1}, used to compute the Gaussian VaR, so as to integrate skewness and kurtosis. This method is also called the modified VaR, and is accurate when asset returns are close to the Gaussian distribution. However, if returns violate the Gaussian assumption significantly, the modified VaR leads to flawed results. The formula for the Cornish–Fisher VaR, CF_VaR, is given as

$$ \text{CF\_VaR} = -\mu(\text{P\&L}) + z_{cf}^{\text{VaR}} \times \sigma(\text{P\&L}) $$

where the only change from the Gaussian VaR is the Cornish–Fisher scaling parameter z_{cf}^{VaR}, defined as

$$ z_{cf}^{\text{VaR}} = z_\alpha + \frac{(z_\alpha^2 - 1)S(\text{P\&L})}{6} + \frac{(z_\alpha^3 - 3z_\alpha)eK(\text{P\&L})}{24} - \frac{(2z_\alpha^3 - 5z_\alpha)S^2(\text{P\&L})}{36} $$

with $z_\alpha = \Phi_\alpha^{-1}$, $S(\text{P\&L})$ the skewness and $eK(\text{P\&L})$ the excess kurtosis of the P&L distribution.[5] When $S = eK = 0$, it is easy to see that we retrieve the Gaussian VaR.

Let us illustrate the modified or Cornish–Fisher VaR with our Google/Amazon portfolio. As is often the case with risk metrics, the calculation seems to be somewhat complicated, but it is not. For the Cornish–Fisher scaling parameter z_{cf}^{VaR}, we use $\alpha = 99\%$ as the confidence level, in order to compare the Cornish–Fisher VaR with the Gaussian VaR computed previously. We need the following inputs:[6]

- $z_{99\%} = \Phi_{99\%}^{-1} = 2.3263$
- $S(\text{P\&L}) = -0.2044$
- $eK(\text{P\&L}) = 6.0111$

We used the SKEW.P( ) and KURT( ) Excel functions to get the values of skewness and excess kurtosis.[7] SKEW.P( ) must be used when the data at hand covers the entire population to be analysed. If you use a sample extracted from a population, the SKEW( ) function should be used instead. We deduce:

$$z_{cf}^{VaR} = 2.3263 + (-0.1504) + 1.4054 + 0.0158$$
$$= 3.5971$$

We observe that z_{cf}^{VaR} is higher than the inverse of the cumulative density function of the standardized normal distribution (or quantile) $\Phi_{99\%}^{-1}$. We have $3.5971 > 2.3263$. This is not surprising, since the former includes both the skewness and excess kurtosis. The Cornish–Fisher VaR is a more conservative risk measure than the Gaussian VaR. To compute the Cornish–Fisher VaR at the 99% confidence level, we need the mean and volatility of the P&L distribution:

- $\mu(\text{P\&L}) = \$50.95$
- $\sigma(\text{P\&L}) = \$1393.52$

We thus have

$$\text{CF\_VaR} = -\mu(\text{P\&L}) + z_{cf}^{VaR} \times \sigma(\text{P\&L})$$
$$= -\$50.95 + (3.5971 \times \$1393.52)$$
$$= \$4961.68$$

For the same Google/Amazon portfolio, we have found a Gaussian VaR of $3190.85. Unsurprisingly, the Cornish–Fisher VaR is higher since it integrates the first four moments of the P&L distribution (mean, standard deviation, skewness and kurtosis), and the Gaussian VaR only the first two (mean and standard deviation). We can also note a negative skewness and a very high excess kurtosis indicating fat tails, as expected for a portfolio of equities. This shows how important skewness and (excess of) kurtosis are in risk management, since the VaR increases by 55% when they are included in the calculation.

The Cornish–Fisher ES follows the same logic as the Cornish–Fisher VaR, even if the scaling parameter is slightly modified:

$$z_{cf}^{Var} = z_\alpha + \frac{(z_\alpha^2 - 1)S(\text{P\&L})}{6} + \frac{(z_\alpha^3 - 3z_\alpha)eK(\text{P\&L})}{24} - \frac{(2z_\alpha^3 - 5z_\alpha)S^2(\text{P\&L})}{36}$$

It follows that (numbers are rounded to four decimal places)

$$z_{cf}^{ES} = 2.3378 \times [0.9207 + 0.9874 + 1.1050]$$

Gaussian ES scaling
factor at 97.5%

$$= 7.0442$$

As for the VaR, we observe that z_{cf}^{ES}, the Cornish–Fisher scaling factor of ES, is higher than its Gaussian counterpart. We have $7.0442 > 2.3378$. Then, we compute the modified ES (Cornish–Fisher) as follows:

$$\begin{aligned} CF\_ES &= -\mu(P\&L) + z_{cf}^{ES} \times \sigma(P\&L) \\ &= -\$50.95 + 7.0442 \times \$1392.52 \\ &= \$9765.21 \end{aligned}$$

The modified ES indicates that if the 97.5% modified or Cornish–Fisher VaR is exceeded (not reproduced here), we will lose on average $9765.21. The large difference between the modified VaR and ES is explained by the high excess kurtosis (fat tails). In order to compare the Gaussian VaR and ES with their Cornish–Fisher counterparts for the Google/Amazon portfolio, we reproduce the results in **Table 20**.

TABLE 20 Gaussian and Cornish–Fisher VaR and ES

	Gaussian	**Cornish–Fisher**
VaR ($\alpha = 99\%$)	$3190.85	$4961.68
ES ($\alpha = 97.5\%$)	$3206.81	$9765.21

NOTES

1. Recall the relationship between covariance (σ_{ij}) and correlation (ρ_{ij}) between assets i and j:

$$\rho_{ij} = \frac{\sigma_{ij}}{\sigma_i \sigma_j} \Rightarrow \sigma_{ij} = \rho_{ij} \times \sigma_i \times \sigma_j$$

2. Another approach to model volatility in risk management is GARCH-type models. GARCH (Generalized Autoregressive Conditional Heteroscedasticity) is referred to as a time series process which models volatility as a function of past returns and past values of volatility.

3. Standardization is a useful scaling method to track data that is otherwise difficult to compare due to different metrics. This is optional here since Google and Amazon stock prices are both expressed in USD, but they operate in different industries. This explains why we use standardized and not raw returns. The tail analysis is not modified with raw returns. The end result of *standardization* is to rescale data to have a mean of zero and a standard deviation of one.

4. Strictly speaking, the expression for kurtosis is

$$\eta^4 = \mathbb{E}\left[\left(r_i - \mu\right)^4\right],$$

which defines the fourth-order centred moment of a distribution. For skewness, we have

$$s^3 = \mathbb{E}\left[\left(r_i - \mu\right)^3\right],$$

which defines the third-order centred moment of a distribution.

5. Should you want to use the skewness and kurtosis of the loss distribution instead, consider the following relationships: $S(L) = -S(P\&L)$ and $K(L) = K(P\&L)$.

6. For the sake of clarity, we report the parameter values rounded to four decimal places, but the calculation of z_{cf} is run with exact values.

7. The Excel function KURT( ) gives the excess kurtosis, which is defined as kurtosis minus 3.

## CHAPTER 12

Ex-Post Evaluation of a Risk Model: Backtesting

Backtesting is an essential part of risk management both from a regulatory and an internal perspective. Backtesting is an ex-post procedure used to check the accuracy of the risk measure/model used by financial institutions. The idea is to compare what the model said in the past with what actually occurred in terms of loss. This explains why it is called "back" testing. We look backward.

As a reminder, to comply with the Basel III regulatory framework (see Part I), a financial institution must compute a daily risk measure over the last 250 trading days or more. With Basel III, the Value-at-Risk (VaR) has been replaced by the Expected Shortfall (ES), a more conservative risk indicator. However, the 99% VaR is still used by the regulator for backtesting purposes, because the ES is much more complicated to backtest than the VaR.[1]

The backtesting procedure is based on a 1-day holding period and compares the 99% VaR with the registered daily Profit and Loss (P&L). As the VaR is used to estimate a potential loss that could be experienced over the next 24 hours, it should not underestimate the realized loss too often to be really helpful in terms of risk management. Of course, the VaR is simply an estimate and, as such, it may provide a wrong estimated loss that is lower than the corresponding realized loss. That said, if the VaR estimate deviates too often from what has been historically observed, it becomes dangerous for a risk manager to ground his risk management policy on such an indicator.

Theoretically speaking, and given the 99% confidence level set by the regulator, the realized loss should not exceed the VaR estimate more than once every 100 observations on average to be consistent. For a given α confidence level, we know that the probability of incurring a loss strictly higher than the VaR is $(1 - \alpha)\%$. This defines the bearable error risk. Above this threshold, there is a problem with the VaR model because it is wrong more often than it should be, still from a theoretical standpoint. In other words, it is not consistent with the specified $\alpha\%$ confidence level.

As mentioned earlier, backtesting makes sense both to the bank and the regulator. For the former, it is a powerful way to check the reliability of its internal risk model and thus have an accurate picture of its risk exposures, as far as possible since the VaR only provides a risk estimate. The regulator focuses on the systemic risk generated by the financial system as a whole, and thus the default probability of each bank within this system. This is where backtesting comes in, to penalize banks whose VaR models fail more frequently than they should.[2]

When the loss exceeds the VaR, the model has failed, and it is called an exception. Backtesting consists in counting the number of exceptions over the last 250 trading days. As the α confidence level is set to 99% in the Basel framework, the probability of observing an exception every trading day is 1%. Depending on the number of exceptions identified, the supervisor will apply a penalty coefficient between 0 and 1.[3]

The ξ ("ksi") penalty coefficient enters into the capital requirement calculation each bank must meet on a daily basis to comply with the Basel III regulatory framework. The ξ coefficient ($0 \leq \xi \leq 0.5$) is added to a constant equal to 1.5 to give the so-called multiplication factor, $m_c = 1.5 + \xi$. The magnitude of the multiplication factor is immediately related to the quality of the internal risk model, with a range between 1.5 and 2. The lower bound corresponds to the best possible outcome from the 1-year backtesting procedure at the bank-wide level, and the upper bond corresponds to the worst one.

The quality of an internal risk model depends on its ex-post performance assessed through the backtesting procedure. The smaller the number of exceptions, the higher the performance, and the lower the multiplication factor. The capital requirement is a regulatory constraint for the bank because this capital amount acts as a buffer to prevent the bank from going into default, should a huge loss occur. The bank's interest is to hold the minimum amount to meet the capital requirement, since in some sense it is frozen capital. That explains why the backtesting outcomes are so important. Through the multiplication factor $m_c = 1.5 + \xi$, there will be a genuine leverage effect on the capital requirement calculation. And the magnitude of this leverage effect depends on the value of the ξ penalty coefficient, which is linked to the ex-post performance of the backtesting procedure.

The Basel Committee defines three colour zones, each corresponding to a number of exceptions identified in a sample based on 250 trading days, such as reported in **Table 21**.

A penalty coefficient ξ set to zero indicates that there is no problem. The number of exceptions ranges from zero—the optimal outcome from a backtesting procedure—to four. The internal VaR model used by the bank is considered good enough not to be penalized by the supervisor.

If the number of exceptions falls into the amber zone (between five and nine exceptions in **Table 21**), the VaR model is not consistent enough with the 99% confidence level due to a high number of exceptions. The VaR model is

TABLE 21 Value of the penalty coefficient ξ in the Basel III framework

Zone	Number of Exceptions	ξ
Green	0–4	0.00
	5	0.20
	6	0.26
Amber	7	0.33
	8	0.38
	9	0.42
Red	10+	0.50

probably consistent with a less demanding confidence level that is lower than 99%. While this is not a big deal, the penalty coefficient is no longer equal to zero and the bank is penalized.

Finally, the red zone defines the worst outcome from a VaR backtesting. The number of exceptions is obviously too high (10+) and as a result the penalty coefficient is set to 0.5, the highest possible value. The model accuracy is weak and the consequences for the bank may be serious as the supervisor can reject the bank's internal risk model.

To illustrate the backtesting procedure, we identify in **Figures 17 and 18** the exceptions occurring during the year 2008 for a long position of $1 m on Google and Amazon. This year was dramatic in terms of VaR over-runs due to the worldwide financial turmoil. To highlight how the risk model can impact the backtesting outcomes, we select the following three VaR methods:

- Historical VaR (non-parametric model)
- Gaussian VaR (parametric model)
- GARCH VaR with $\lambda = 0.94$ (model developed by RiskMetrics™)

These three VaR methods are estimated for a 1-day holding period at the 99% confidence level. We talked about the RiskMetrics model briefly in the last chapter, when discussing volatility modelling. The RiskMetrics approach is grounded on an econometric model called Exponential Weighted Moving Average (EWMA). In short, this model integrates a decay factor λ (≤ 1), which allows for allocating a greater weighting to the most recent observations. As a result, the data point $t - i - 1$ is weighted less than the data point $t - i$. The decay factor $\lambda = 0.94$ is used for daily data.

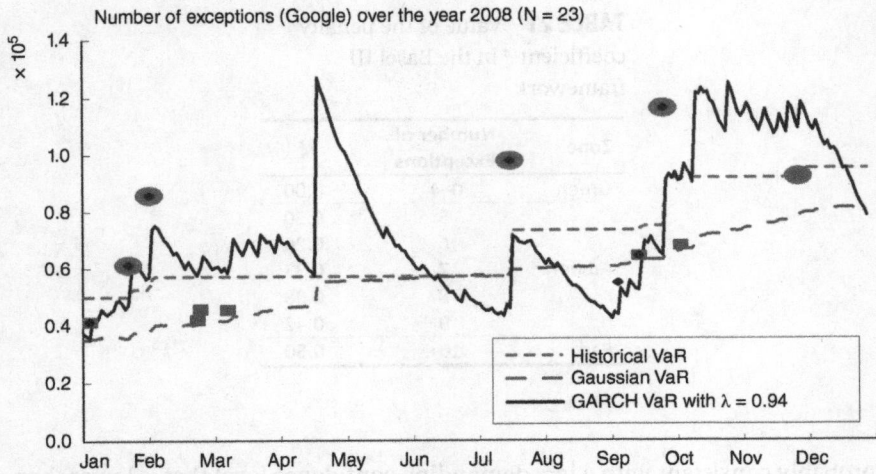

FIGURE 17   Number of exceptions for Google in 2008

The RiskMetrics model is a specific case of a GARCH process. This class of econometric models was first initiated by Tim Bollerslev, a PhD student (see Bollerslev, 1986). The core idea was to relax a very demanding assumption about volatility, called "homoscedasticity". Technically speaking, for a short while, this assumption indicates that the residuals of a time series model have a constant variance. Of course, this property is never verified when considering economic or financial time series, whose variance is not constant and homogeneous through time. This feature defines a heteroscedastic process.

In **Figure 17**, each symbol represents an exception (the VaR underestimated the realized loss) and is related to one of the three VaR methods under review. The total number of exceptions for Google in 2008 was 23, of which 5 were due to historical VaR, 11 to Gaussian VaR and 7 to GARCH VaR. Four distinct situations are displayed in **Figure 17**, each indicated by a specific symbol:

● indicates an exception generated by the three VaR methods under review, for example on 17 July 2008 or 26 September 2008.

▩ indicates an exception generated by two VaR methods, since there are two different shapes in this symbol: a circle for the historical VaR and a square for the Gaussian VaR (28 November 2008).

◆ indicates an exception generated by the Gaussian VaR (square) and the GARCH VaR (diamond). Two dates correspond to this situation: 3 January 2008 and 16 September 2008.

■ indicates an exception generated by the Gaussian VaR exclusively.

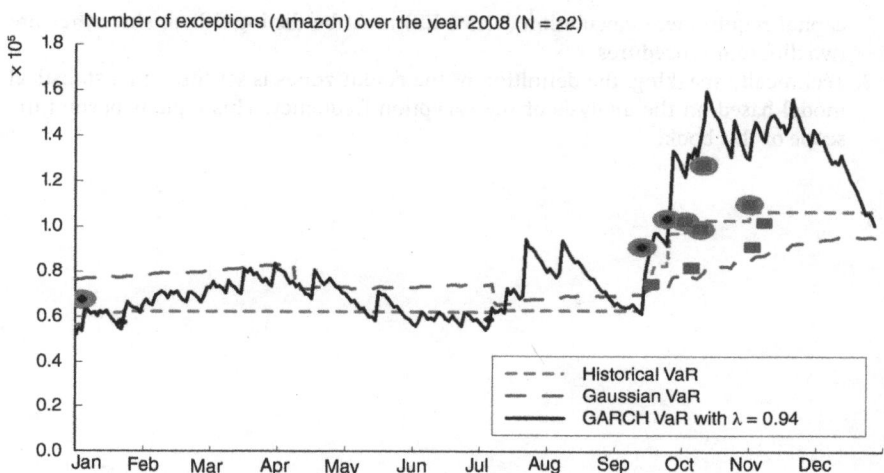

FIGURE 18   Number of exceptions for Amazon in 2008

Surprisingly, the historical VaR outperforms the GARCH VaR. It is common to have a lower number of exceptions with the latter, since it is more dynamic per se. **Figure 18** displays the backtesting of Amazon over the same time period. The total number of exceptions is 22. The breakdown of this total is 7 for historical VaR, 10 for Gaussian VaR and only 5 for GARCH VaR.

The circle and diamond symbol in **Figure 18** indicates an exception occurring on 3 January 2008 and generated both by the historical and GARCH VaR. It is worth noting that the exceptions for Amazon are concentrated in the last quarter of 2008, from 16 September 2008 precisely. This backtesting outcome differs significantly from that of Google, where exceptions occurred throughout the year. We thus obtain different backtesting profiles from Google and Amazon, despite their total number of exceptions being almost equal (22 against 23 for Google and Amazon, respectively). This reinforces the interest of plotting a backtesting procedure.

NOTES

1. This is due to the fact that the ES is not "elicitable", as opposed to the VaR. If a risk measure is elicitable, then there exists a scoring function for that risk measure that can be used for comparative tests on models, making backtesting considerably easier.
2. It should be noted that the 1-year backtesting procedure is still based on the daily 99% VaR model in the Basel III regulatory framework. The 97.5% ES is used to compute the capital requirement for modellable risk factors. Backtesting (99% VaR) and

capital requirement calculation (97.5% ES) must be distinguished, since they are two different procedures.

3. Technically speaking, the definition of the colour zones is set through a statistical model based on the analysis of the exception frequency. This topic is beyond the scope of this book.

## CHAPTER 13

A Forward-Looking Evaluation of Risk: Stress Testing

THE RETURN PERIOD

The concept of a rare or extreme event is at the core of stress testing. As we mentioned previously, the probability of occurrence is very low but still higher than expected in a Gaussian framework. The problem with this definition of an extreme event is its lack of precision. What does a "low probability" mean exactly? What is the threshold for considering a probability as low? Answering these two questions is of crucial importance for risk management, specifically to compare two events.

The statistician Emil Julius Gumbel offered an interesting alternative to cope with extreme events: the return period (Gumbel, 1958). Initially developed outside the field of risk management (e.g., hydrology and flood prediction), the return period is commonly used nowadays in stress-testing programmes to express the frequency of occurrence of an event. The return period is defined as the average wait time between the exceedance of a specified extreme threshold. It is denoted as $\breve{t}(x)$, where x stands for the threshold.

Because an extreme loss may threaten the strength of a bank, the return period of such a rare event might be 100 years, corresponding to a probability of occurrence of 1% in any year. A common misinterpretation is to conclude that if this extreme loss with a 100-year return period occurs, the next one will occur in about 100 years. It is wrong to think that such an event will not occur again in your lifetime. Actually, a similar extreme loss has a 1% probability of occurring again in any year, regardless of when the last similar loss occurred. We can only conclude that it is 10 times less likely to occur than an extreme loss with a return period of 10 years (or a probability of 10%). The return period is defined as follows:

$$\breve{t}(x) = \frac{1}{1 - F(x)}$$

where $1 - F(x)$ is the probability of a value being equal to or exceeding x. Its reciprocal defines the return period. When applying this definition to the Value-at-Risk (VaR), we have

$$\breve{t}(\text{VaR}) = \frac{1}{1 - F(F^{-1}(x))} = \frac{1}{1 - \alpha}$$

As a reminder:
$$\text{VaR} = F^{-1}(\alpha)$$

where F is the losses distribution and α is the confidence level. In this equation, we just replace x by the definition of VaR. We report in **Table 22** the return periods for Google calculated under the Gaussian assumption from 2004-08-19 to 2022-02-17.[1]

These return periods are not really useful for a risk manager. How do we interpret a return period expressed in millions or billions of years? What kind of risk limits could be grounded on such figures? Even when talking about extreme risk events that could expose the bank or financial institution to bankruptcy, for which very high return periods are required, it seems difficult to exploit these results meaningfully. This is due to the Gaussian assumption about Google's returns, which is wrong (we know that the Gaussian assumption largely underestimates extreme events).

We should obtain more realistic return periods by using a probability distribution able to take what happens in the tails into account. Such a distribution is called Generalized Extreme Value (GEV). Interestingly, among its three parameters, one is linked to the tail of the distribution (in our case, financial returns). This is a great improvement on the Gaussian distribution, which does not own such a parameter. When computing a GEV VaR, we compute a parametric VaR (like the Gaussian VaR) focused exclusively on the tail distribution (strongly underestimated by the Gaussian VaR). The same obviously holds true when working with returns, be they negative or positive. With the GEV distribution, we are at the core of the tail distribution.

TABLE 22 Return periods (in years) of Google in a Gaussian setting

	Date	$r(t)$	$\breve{t}$	Date	$r(t)$	$\breve{t}$
#1	2020-03-16	−12.36%	2.5×10^8	2008-04-18	18.22%	2.8×10^{19}
#2	2008-09-29	−12.34%	2.2×10^8	2015-07-17	15.06%	6.4×10^{12}
#3	2008-07-18	−10.28%	2.1×10^5	2004-10-22	14.35%	3.0×10^{11}
#4	2008-12-01	−9.65%	3.3×10^4	2008-10-13	13.77%	2.8×10^{10}
#5	2008-02-01	−8.96%	4.8×10^3	2013-10-18	12.92%	1.0×10^9

Another way to cope with return periods in a GEV framework, is to set different return periods $\check{t}$ and estimate the underlying event corresponding to each of these return periods. As we are interested in building stress scenarios corresponding to crisis periods, we use pretty high return periods from a risk management perspective (e.g., 5 to 100 years). The advantage of this alternative is to provide a risk manager with operational results, in contrast to the return periods in **Table 22**.

Let us consider the two assets, Google and Amazon, we have in the portfolio from 2004-08-19 to 2022-02-17. In **Table 23**, we display the daily stress scenarios of Google and Amazon estimated through a GEV setting for long and short positions.[2]

- We observe that the severity (magnitude) of the stress scenario is higher for Amazon than Google, regardless of the return period $\check{t}$ under review. We also report in **Table 23** the extreme statistics (minimum and maximum daily returns) and the associated return period $\check{t}^*$, expressed in years. **Figure 19** plots the results reported in **Table 23**.
- Part of these results highlight a shortcoming of the GEV method. It is very unlikely to observe a decrease in stock prices of Google or Amazon by more than 30% on a given day. Their listing on the stock market would probably be suspended before. That said, we do not know what the time horizon of a crisis scenario should be. Is a 1-day scenario more or less relevant than a 10-day or a 1-month scenario? Difficult to say.

Up to now we have worked with univariate stress scenarios, meaning that the return periods displayed in **Table 23** are also univariate. This term indicates that we have no idea about the joint effect of a decrease in the stock

TABLE 23   Stress scenarios (in %) of Google and Amazon

	Long Position		Short Position	
Return Period $\check{t}$	**Google**	**Amazon**	**Google**	**Amazon**
5	−10.64	−14.78	13.50	18.51
10	−12.91	−18.85	17.95	24.72
25	−16.45	−25.74	26.11	36.07
50	−19.61	−32.42	34.63	47.92
75	−21.67	−37.04	40.84	56.55
100	−23.25	−40.68	45.90	63.58
Extreme statistic	−12.37	−24.62	18.23	23.86
$\check{t}^*$	8.55	21.89	10.37	9.19

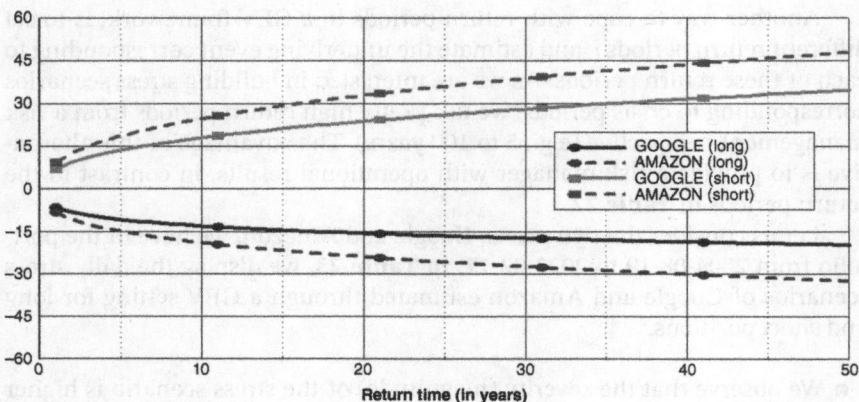

FIGURE 19   Stress scenarios (in %) of Google and Amazon

prices of Google and Amazon during a turmoil period. We are just able to estimate the isolated outcome expressed in terms of a decrease in their respective stock prices (**Table 23**, in %) under a crisis scenario defined from different return periods (**Table 23**, $\check{t}$ as number of years).

As we hold a portfolio encompassing both Google and Amazon, it should make sense to simulate a crisis period (e.g., a decrease by 10% in the stock prices of the two assets) and then calculate the corresponding return periods. Let's start with the unidimensional return periods. We have the following:

	Google	Amazon
$\check{t}$	2.35	1.09

We observe that both return periods are very short, a little bit more than 2 years for Google. To compute the underlying return period corresponding to a joint decrease by 10%, first of all we need to model the dependence between the two asset returns. With this aim, we can use a standard tool in finance called copulas.[3] The return period for the pair (Google, Amazon) is 29.25 years.

We understand better now why building bivariate stress scenarios from univariate stress scenarios is totally irrelevant. Adding the Google and Amazon return periods to obtain the bivariate (Google, Amazon) return period is the worst idea. We obtain a return period of $2.35 + 1.09 = 5.79$ years, which is significantly lower than 29.25 years. The take-home message is that the dependence structure between two assets impacts the return period estimation significantly.

HISTORICAL STRESS SCENARIOS

This class of stress tests is similar to the historical VaR, since it is grounded on historical values of risk factors. The basic idea is to identify the worst period for a specific risk factor (e.g., equities). To implement historical stress scenarios, we have to build the so-called loss function, defined as follows:

$$\mathcal{L}(h) = \min_t R(t; h)$$

where $R(t; h)$ is the asset return for the period $[t, t + h]$. This is also called the drawdown function. The maximum drawdown refers to the maximum loss and may thus be considered the expected worst-case risk scenario. It is calculated as follows:[4]

$$\text{MDD} = \underset{\Delta t}{\min} \mathcal{L}(\Delta t)$$

The time period Δt is expressed in number of trading days. Therefore, setting $\Delta t = 5$ corresponds to a weekly stress scenario and $\Delta t = 20$ corresponds to a monthly stress (no trading activity on Saturday and Sunday). Obviously, we set $\Delta t = 1$ to obtain a daily stress. To illustrate, **Figure 20** reports the daily drawdown function $\mathcal{L}(h)$ of Google for the year 2008.

From **Table 24**, we know that the maximum drawdown for Google is −65.29% and occurred between 6 November 2007 and 24 November 2008. The maximum drawdown for Amazon is almost equal to Google's (−65.25%)

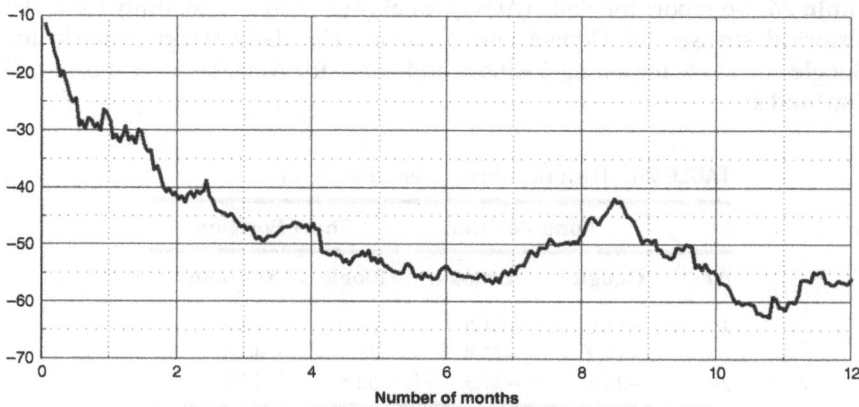

FIGURE 20   Loss function of Google (year 2008)

TABLE 24 Drawdowns derived from Figure 20

	Google			Amazon		
#1	2007-11-06	2008-11-24	−65.29%	2007-10-23	2008-11-20	−65.25%
#2	2006-01-11	2006-03-13	−28.53%	2005-12-13	2006-08-11	−47.33%
#3	2005-02-03	2005-03-14	−17.01%	2004-12-30	2005-04-27	−29.46%

TABLE 25 Worst historical losses of Google (in %)

	1 day		1 week		1 month	
#1	2020-03-16	−11.63	2008-10-08	−17.88	2020-03-20	−29.58
#2	2008-09-29	−11.61	2008-11-20	−16.83	2008-11-20	−27.02
#3	2008-07-18	−9.77	2020-03-12	−15.46	2006-02-15	−26.70
#4	2008-12-01	−9.21	2008-11-11	−15.12	2008-02-01	−24.72
#5	2008-02-01	−8.58	2006-02-07	−14.96	2008-10-10	−23.46

and occurred during a similar period of time (between 23 October 2007 and 20 November 2008).

In **Table 25**, we report the five maximum losses for Google from 19 August 2004 to 2 February 2022 for different time horizons (1, 5, 20 days).

The maximum daily drawdown is −11.63%, reached on 16 March 2020. Then, we have four drawdowns that correspond to lower losses. Note that there are many drawdowns over a period of time, but only one maximum drawdown.

It is also relevant to build historical stress scenarios for different time periods Δt, as explained before, and for both long and short positions. In **Table 26**, we report the daily ($\Delta t = 1$), weekly ($\Delta t = 5$) and monthly ($\Delta t = 20$) historical stresses for Google and Amazon. The daily stress scenario for Google is −11.6% for a long position, and 26.9% for Amazon for a short position, and so on.

TABLE 26 Historical stress scenarios (in %)

	Long Position		Short Position	
Δt	Google	Amazon	Google	Amazon
1	−11.6	−21.8	20.0	26.9
5	−17.9	−23.8	32.4	40.6
20	−29.3	−37.5	58.5	57.7

TABLE 27   Baseline stress scenarios (in %)

	Long Position		Short Position	
Δt	**Google**	**Amazon**	**Google**	**Amazon**
1	−10	−20	20	25
5	−20	−25	30	40
20	−30	−40	60	60

Such results are interesting as they can be used as a baseline stress scenario, such as those reported in **Table 27**, where we simply round up or down the results from **Table 26**. This approach may seem to be subjective. It is. It should be noted, however, that the baseline stress scenarios in **Table 27** are grounded on historical events that occurred in the past. This explains why the historical approach of stress testing is said to be objective.

NOTES

1. We obtain similar return periods for Amazon.
2. The size of blocks is equal to 20 trading days (about 1 month of trading). Returns are calculated daily and the short and long positions are modelled using the block maxima and the block minima.
3. Dependence modelling is a technical topic beyond the scope of this book. In short, a copula function is a statistical tool that generalizes the well-known coefficient of correlation in a non-Gaussian universe. The interested reader can refer to Nelsen (2006).
4. This formula holds for a long position. For a short position, the loss function is defined as the opposite: $\mathcal{L}(h) = \max_t R(t; h)$.

Three

Getting Conduct Risk to Scale

Conduct risk is best defined as a set of expected behaviours. It is, of course, directly related to misconduct, which can generally be understood as conduct that falls short of expected standards, including legal, professional, internal conduct and ethical standards—according to the Financial Stability Board (FSB). Conduct risk events are a source of potential harm; they can damage a firm's reputation/brand and could lead to fines, in addition to the cost of the misconduct breach itself.

In this third and last part of the book, we start by providing readers with an overview of conduct risk, with a focus on its definition and scope. Then, we identify some conduct risk markers from recent financial disasters due to misconduct and wrongdoings. A first method to calculate a conduct risk score is offered, and we show how to implement these markers into a conduct indicator. This conduct risk score may be considered as an initial step to foster a culture of appropriate conduct outcomes in financial institutions.

The last three chapters of this part are dedicated to a fuller picture of conduct risk, centred around a risk-taker's conduct risk index, through a worked example. Hot questions still pending about this conduct risk index and tentative answers are then provided. Lastly, we try to identify and understand the root causes of poor conduct.

## CHAPTER 14

The Big Picture of Conduct Risk

To tackle the causes and consequences of misconduct, the Financial Stability Board (FSB) published, in April 2018, a toolkit to promote incentives for good behaviour.[1] This work identifies three overarching areas for mitigating misconduct from a financial stability perspective: (1) cultural drivers of misconduct; (2) individual responsibility and accountability; and (3) the "rolling bad apples" phenomenon. To the best of our knowledge, this is the first time the "rolling bad apples" phenomenon has been considered as a factor of misconduct. This represents real progress because it prevents the movement of "bad apples" (employees with a history of misconduct) within or between firms.

Recognizing that firms—while they have a collective identity—are made up of their individuals, the Financial Conduct Authority (FCA) launched, in 2016, the Senior Managers and Certification Regime (SM&CR).[2] The regime was adopted by the banking sector in 2016, then by insurers and finally extended to around 47000 FCA-regulated firms. The certification element of the regime applies to more junior staff who are nonetheless risk-takers. The FCA explains that the SM&CR "*aims to reduce harm to consumers and strengthen market integrity by making individuals more accountable for conduct and competence*".[3] The purpose is thus to embed responsibility and accountability. As part of this, the SM&CR aims to:

- Encourage staff to take personal responsibility for their actions.
- Improve conduct at all levels.
- Make sure firms and staff clearly understand and can show who does what.

According to Andrew Bailey, Chief Executive Officer of the FCA from 2016 to 2020, the SM&CR is intended "*to identify individual responsibility—not at the expense of collective responsibility but alongside it—and increase individual accountability, not least as a contributor to stronger culture and governance*".[4]

While the introduction of the SM&CR does not require firms to change their governance structure or hire new people to fill specific roles, the most senior people in a firm who perform key roles must be approved by the regulators as fit and proper to carry out the responsibilities before starting their roles. The Fit & Proper test developed by the FCA sets out detailed guidance about the types of things firms should consider as part of assessing a person's fitness and propriety.[5] This includes:

- Honesty, integrity and reputation.
- Competence and capability, including whether the person satisfies any relevant FCA training and competence requirements.
- Financial soundness.

Every senior management function holder must have a *"Statement of Responsibility that clearly states what they are responsible and accountable for [.../...] and will have a Duty of Responsibility under the Financial Services and Markets Act 2000"*. This means that senior managers should know what they are responsible for, but it also means that the map of responsibility should go right across the firm. Senior Management Functions (SMFs) include any senior people performing key roles in a firm. The combined list of FCA and PRA (Prudential Regulation Authority) SMFs is displayed in **Appendix 2**. SMFs must report to the FCA within 7 days of concluding disciplinary action for a conduct rule breach. For non-SMF staff subject to the conduct rules, the number of conduct rule breaches is reported on a yearly basis.

In March 2023, the FCA updated the minimum standards of individual behaviour in financial services:

1. You must act with integrity.
2. You must act with due skill, care and diligence.
3. You must be open and cooperative with the FCA, the PRA and other regulators.[6]
4. You must pay due regard to the interests of customers and treat them fairly.
5. You must observe proper standards of market conduct.

In July 2023, the Consumer Duty set higher and clearer standards of consumer protection across financial services and required firms to put their customers' needs first. This includes a sixth individual conduct rule requiring all conduct rule staff to *"act to deliver good outcomes for retail customers"*. This new conduct rule is related to misconduct events such as unsuitable advice to customers, illegal credit card practices or the mis-selling of PPI (Payment Protection Insurance) in the UK. In September 2019, Lloyds and Barclays were hit by $4bn of insurance mis-selling claims provision. Lloyds disclosed later that it had set aside up to an extra £1.8bn ($2.2bn at the time) to settle PPI claims, while Barclays said later that it had set aside between £1.2 and £1.6bn.

TABLE 28   Conduct rules

Positive Indicators	Negative Indicators
■ Relevant SMF can demonstrate appropriate involvement in/oversight of training.	■ Relevant SMF has limited knowledge of training approach and/or has delegated with limited oversight.
■ Training is interactive and uses realistic scenarios.	■ Simple computer-based training only—with little attempt to tailor to role.
■ Examples/scenarios draw out nuances of how the rules apply to each type of role.	■ Training only gives obvious examples of breaches—for example, fraud or not attending mandatory training—which do not draw out nuances.
■ Line managers are involved in training delivery, not just HR or a project team.	■ Training is delivered by an HR, compliance or a project team with no line management involvement.
■ Training is reinforced regularly and built into on-boarding.	■ Training is a one-off exercise and/or not built into on-boarding.
■ Effectiveness of Conduct Rules training is assessed.	■ No measures of the effectiveness of Conduct Rules training.
■ Training is put in the context of the overall regime.	■ Training is not put in the context of the overall regime.
■ Regime/Conduct Rules are presented as a step change in regulatory expectations.	■ Regime/Conduct Rules are presented as nothing new, simply "what we do already".
■ Conduct is linked to F&P and performance assessments.	■ Conduct is not linked to F&P or performance assessments.

Source: https://www.fca.org.uk/firms/senior-managers-and-certification-regime/conduct-rules
SMF: Senior Management Function
F&P: fit and proper individuals who must be approved as such by the regulators (FCA and PRA) to do their job

Central to the SM&CR is to provide conduct rules staff with training to understand what these rules mean for them. As observed by Patricia Jackson, Adviser on Risk Governance EMEIA at EY: *"if you go down the ethics training route, it has to be explicit case-study based training, so that when issues come up people know exactly what to do"*.[7] Training is a key feature of the conduct rules defined by the SM&CR. They are displayed in **Table 28**. Further information about the conduct rules listed is contained in the Code of Conduct sourcebook (COCON) in the FCA Handbook.[8]

Looking into the future, and despite the efforts undertaken by the FCA, we argue that risk management is still insufficiently focused on culture and behaviours. That is especially surprising given that most losses experienced by the banking industry in the last 15 years have largely been caused by misconduct and culture issues.

The commonly used risk indicators were and still are inefficient in identifying early warning signals of misconduct by key players—not in the sense of outright personal profits, but in the sense of putting the institution at risk. Risk management should shift from purely financial risk metrics to the monitoring of human behaviours.

NOTES

1. See FSB (2018).
2. The FCA regulates financial services firms and financial markets in the UK.
3. Source: https://www.fca.org.uk/firms/senior-managers-certification-regime (first published 5 July 2015; last updated 30 March 2023).
4. *The Importance of Diversity*, speech by Andrew Bailey at the PIMFA Wealth of Diversity Conference. Source: https://www.fca.org.uk/news/speeches/importance-diversity (first published 5 February 2019; last updated 8 February 2019).
5. See FCA (2019, p. 40). Available at https://www.fca.org.uk/publication/policy/guide-for-fca-solo-regulated-firms.pdf
6. The PRA is part of the Bank of England and responsible for the prudential regulation and supervision of banks, building societies, credit unions, insurers and major investment firms.
7. From regulation to results: Bank strategy. *The Banker*, Special Report, January 2015, p. 9.
8. https://www.handbook.fca.org.uk/handbook/COCON/1/

## CHAPTER 15

Markers of Conduct Risk

Since the aftermath of the 2008 financial turmoil, there have been numerous instances of financial disasters and wrongdoings. Poor conduct and misbehaviour persist in the financial services industry. This probably explains why the UK Financial Conduct Authority (FCA) aims to reduce and prevent financial crime and fraud from happening in the first place, delivering assertive actions on market abuse.[1]

This lack of progress in improving conduct indicates that the risk indicators used are inefficient at predicting such disasters, and traditional actions are unable to avoid their repetition. Each time a new financial scandal occurs, the same risk management platitudes are offered to clean up after the disaster:

- Improve compliance and risk management functions.
- Hire additional resources to ensure sufficient skills and expertise are in place to prevent financial wrongdoings.
- Invest in more effective IT systems for automated transactions monitoring.
- Create committees to improve the board's oversight of compliance issues.
- Overhaul the sanctions screening techniques to better detect suspect accounts and transactions, and so on.

The multi-faceted nature of conduct risk explains why there is no one-size-fits-all framework that can be implemented to assess if the firm is conducting its business responsibly. **Figure 21** illustrates the wide-ranging nature of conduct risk and describes different types or markers of poor conduct that still plague managements, boards, regulators, industry stakeholders and the public at large.

Without going into details about the story behind each example of poor conduct in **Figure 21**, the Danske Bank's money laundering scandal is remarkable as it might only be the "tip of the iceberg"; investigators should scrutinize major Western banks.

- *Money laundering.* The Danske Bank's money laundering scandal provides evidence of hidden misconduct inside a financial institution. Between 2007 and 2015, an astonishing $227bn of improper money

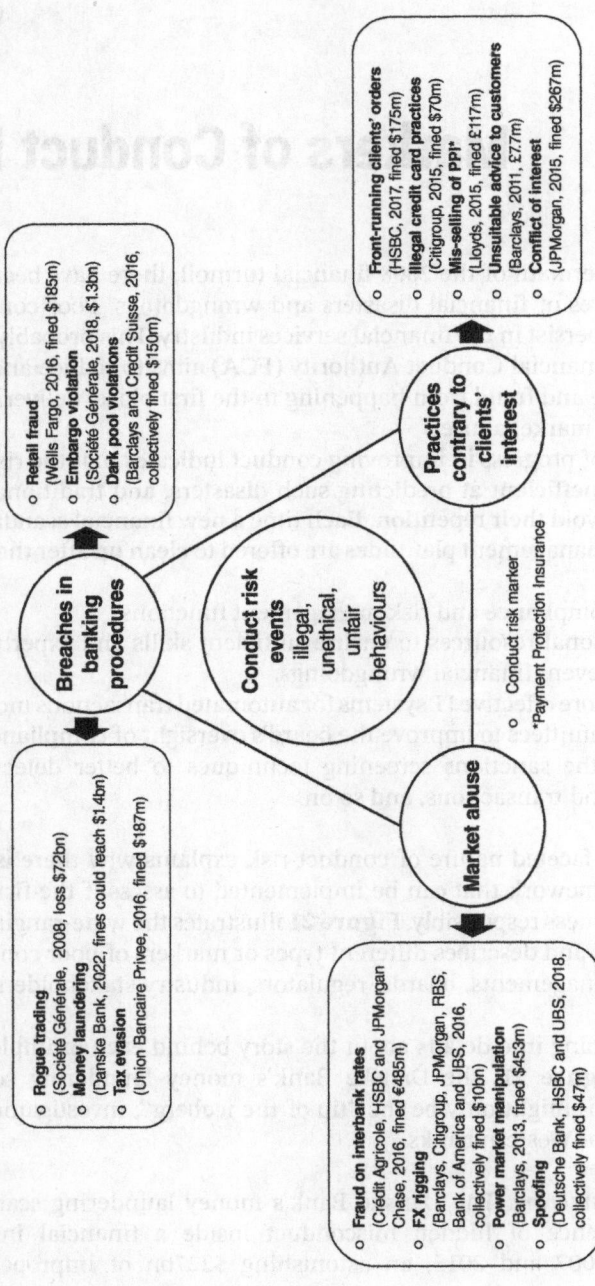

Breaches in banking procedures

- o **Retail fraud**
  (Wells Fargo, 2016, fined $185m)
- o **Embargo violation**
  (Société Générale, 2018, $1.3bn)
- o **Dark pool violations**
  (Barclays and Credit Suisse, 2016, collectively fined $150m)

Practices contrary to clients' interest

- o **Front-running clients' orders**
  (HSBC, 2017, fined $175m)
- o **Illegal credit card practices**
  (Citigroup, 2015, fined $70m)
- o **Mis-selling of PPI***
  (Lloyds, 2015, fined £117m)
- o **Unsuitable advice to customers**
  (Barclays, 2011, £7.7m)
- o **Conflict of interest**
  (JPMorgan, 2015, fined $267m)

Conduct risk events illegal, unethical, unfair behaviours

- o Conduct risk marker
- o *Payment Protection Insurance

Market abuse

- o **Fraud on interbank rates**
  (Crédit Agricole, HSBC and JPMorgan Chase, 2016, fined €485m)
- o **FX rigging**
  (Barclays, Citigroup, JPMorgan, RBS, Bank of America and UBS, 2016, collectively fined $10bn)
- o **Power market manipulation**
  (Barclays, 2013, fined $453m)
- o **Spoofing**
  (Deutsche Bank, HSBC and UBS, 2018, collectively fined $47m)

FIGURE 21 Markers of conduct risk

flowed through the "non-resident" portfolio of its Estonian branch. The investigation found that the branch operated independently from the rest of the group without adequate control or management attention.

The Danske Bank's scandal reveals that the number of "non-resident" customers and the degree of independence of overseas subsidiaries from the group could be used in the future as money laundering red flags inside a banking network.

- *Retail fraud.* In September 2016, Wells Fargo paid $185m to settle charges that thousands of employees had fraudulently created more than two million deposit and credit card accounts in order to achieve performance targets and earn bonuses. This resulted in customers getting charged fees for services they did not seek, according to the regulators. Los Angeles City Attorney Mike Feuer accused Wells Fargo of high-pressure quotas for workers that encouraged them to skirt the rules.

The Wells Fargo scandal shows there is a need to couple performance targets and bonuses with behavioural patterns to avoid practices contrary to clients' interests. When employees face the threat of being fired if they do not meet unreasonable sales quotas every day, it opens the door to all kinds of misconduct. Mis-selling of PPI (Payment Protection Insurance) in the UK—involving HSBC, Lloyds TSB and Royal Bank of Scotland—is another proof of evidence. Checking that products are appropriate for the customers to whom they are sold should be the starting point of any commercial relationship. Both natural risk-takers like traders and non-Profit and Loss (P&L) employees should not be put in situations where they need to balance increasing their revenues against taking care of their clients' interests.

As they manage their own P&L account, natural risk-takers can potentially modify the aggregate risk profile of a bank. Therefore, their risk appetite should be closely monitored. Avoiding the confusion of roles and responsibilities—front, middle and back office in the hands of a single trader—can obviously help. Moreover, natural risk-takers react to volatility and losses differently from other employees. They can take even riskier positions to offset losses or liquidate large positions and unfavourably move the market. This was the case when Société Générale uncovered the €6.25 billion of losses of the trader Kerviel and liquidated all of them on Martin Luther King Jr Day, when the US markets were closed.

Last, it is also important to detect abnormal behaviours such as oversized need for peer recognition, reluctance to take vacation leave or working solo. The rogue trading scandal at Société Générale has demonstrated that these are early warning signals of potential misconduct. Other well-known examples in the financial services industry, not reported in **Figure 21**, include:

- *Rogue trading.* In 2012, the JPMorgan Chase "London Whale" trading scandal (approximately $5.8bn loss), coupled with an accounting fraud, a massive market manipulation and a unique media manipulation, was centred about a "tranche book" that was trading credit derivatives and credit default swaps of massive size. This book, managed by a business unit called the Chief Investment Officer, was supposed to be a "strategic protection" of the bank.
- *Market manipulation scheme.* Sung Kook (Bill) Hwang—the Founder and Head of Archegos—and three others were charged with racketeering and fraud offences related to a market manipulation scheme.[2] Credit Suisse, among other multinational banking groups, had reached at some point an extraordinary exposure of more than $20bn to the family office Archegos Capital. The board members of the Swiss bank were not aware of this amazing exposure until a few days before the meltdown of Archegos, generating cumulative losses of more than $10bn.

The H20 Asset Management (H20 AM) scandal is not easy to classify in one of the conduct markers displayed in **Figure 21** ("Practices contrary to clients' interest" may be a suitable one), but it is symptomatic of a lack of transparency that leads to conduct breaches. Natixis, a subsidiary of Group BPCE (the second largest banking group in France), informed its clients in 2020 of its decision to cease its partnership with H20 AM, a hedge fund which had previously posted large returns. This was a collateral effect of the on-going scandal after H20 AM put more than $1.2bn of investors' money into illiquid bonds. The amount was over three times the limit.

As observed by Helyette Geman, a research professor in mathematical finance at Johns Hopkins University, it was not simply a flawed calculation of Value-at-Risk or Expected Shortfall that triggered financial disasters. All banks had excellent quant teams, complemented by fully fledged departments of model validation. It was due to a gigantic exposure to a single entity and/or activity, be it a remote branch in the Baltic in the case of Danske Bank, a hedge fund or a family office in the case of Natixis and Credit Suisse, or a single trader managing a large family of financial contracts in the case of JPMorgan. The size of exposure matters greatly, particularly in the situation of market incompleteness, and should be monitored carefully.[3]

NOTES

1. Source: https://www.fca.org.uk/publication/corporate/our-strategy-2022-25.pdf
2. U.S. Department of Justice, Office of Public Affairs, Press Release No. 22-437, Wednesday 27 April 2022.
3. In an incomplete market, not all states of nature can be spanned, and as a result, parties are not able to move funds freely across time and space, nor to manage risk (Tufano, 2003).

## CHAPTER 16

Worked Example 7: Building a Conduct Risk Score

Building a Conduct Risk Score (CRS) from the conduct risk markers in **Figure 21** should not be a goal per se. The customization of a CRS takes central stage in the assessment of how a firm behaves. It is obviously impossible to identify a comprehensive list of conduct risk markers applicable to all banking institutions worldwide. While **Figure 21** may provide some help in building a CRS, identifying conduct risk markers is simply the initial step in building a CRS. The idea is to include into a CRS some of the main issues that are before the banking industry nowadays.

With this in mind, we develop in this section a first example of a CRS allowing a conduct risk event, once identified, to be evaluated individually based on four assessment criteria: (i) impact; (ii) warning time; (iii) duration; and (iv) reactivity. Following our own recommendation to customize a CRS, we reorganize **Figure 21** according to four conduct risk pillars, each related to three conduct risk markers (misconduct event). The three-stage method to calculate our first CRS is displayed in **Figure 22**.

MATCHING RISK MARKERS WITH CONDUCT RISK PILLARS

The identification of conduct risk markers (Step 1 in **Figure 22**) is not so easy given the huge number of potential misconduct events that can arise within a banking institution. As a rule of thumb, even though not wholly satisfactory, it is possible to start with conduct risk markers that may lead (or led in the past) to fines. However, the main difficulty in Step 1 is not the selection of conduct risk markers, but to define the conduct risk pillars in **Figure 22** and then assign each conduct risk marker to the relevant risk pillar. Sometimes the borderline is thin and it becomes difficult to avoid overlapping.

The second step in **Figure 22** consists in defining a set of assessment criteria, in our example impact, warning time, duration and reactivity. Then, each conduct risk marker identified in Step 1 is assessed on a four-level risk scale specific to each criterion of assessment, with specific index values defining

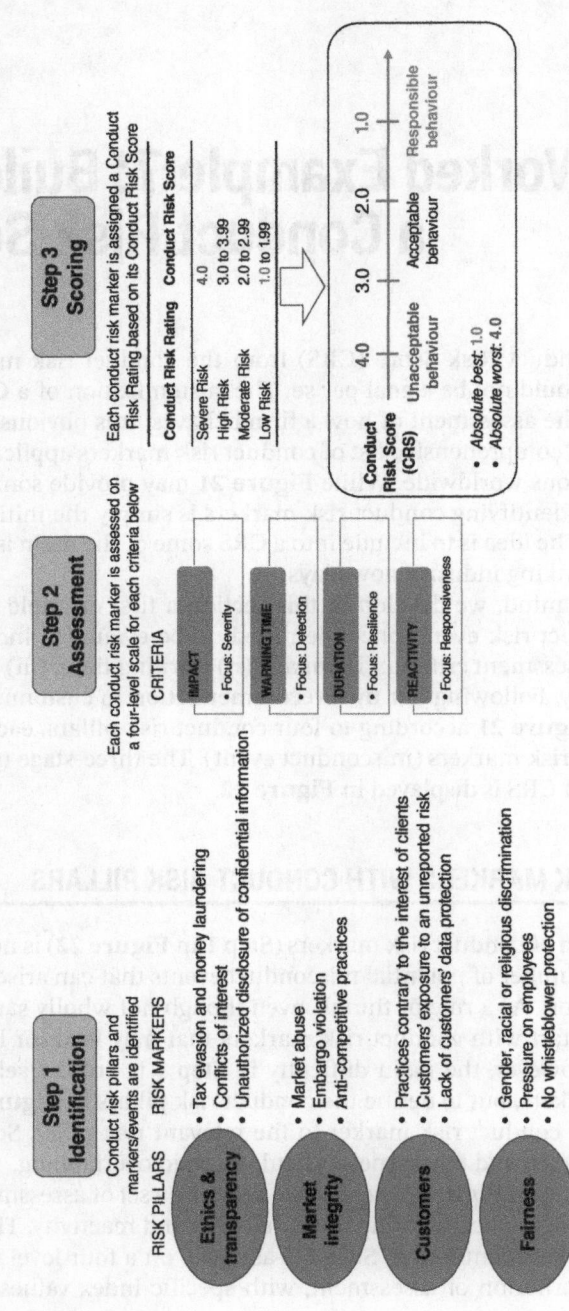

FIGURE 22 Calculation of a Conduct Risk Score (CRS)

each level. Some thresholds are provided to help in this task. Both the number of criteria and the criteria themselves can be tailored to the specific needs of a given financial institution, as described further below. In this first example, we use the following four assessment criteria:

- *Impact.* The overall impact a conduct breach may have on a bank's profitability and/or its reputation. Here, the focus is the severity or magnitude of impact.
- *Warning time.* The amount of time between the initial warning and the occurrence of a conduct breach. The focus is the detection of a weak signal.
- *Duration.* The length of time the direct effects of a conduct breach on a bank's profitability and reputation may remain active. This focus is the resilience of a banking institution. Duration evaluates (only indirectly) a bank's ability to recover from conduct risk breaches. The underlying assumption is that it should be easier to recover from a marginal conduct breach than a long-lasting one. To some extent, this is obviously linked to the bank's resilience.
- *Reactivity.* The responsiveness level of a bank to a conduct breach. Reactivity assesses the speed at which a bank can effectively respond to a conduct breach. The focus is thus the responsiveness of the banking institution.

To illustrate this second step, let's take the example of *Impact*, the first assessment criterion defined above, and *market abuse*, a conduct risk marker related to the conduct risk pillar labelled "Market integrity" in **Figure 22**. We are interested in assessing *market abuse* on the four-level risk scale, to then derive the index value of this conduct risk marker. This process is summarized in **Figure 23**; it holds true regardless of the conduct risk marker under review. Interestingly, it can equally be used with historical data or in a predictive way. In the former case, the resulting CRS in **Figure 22** will give a picture of the past only, which could be used as a baseline scenario to anticipate the future. To put it differently, given our last year's bad CRS, how could we act more responsibly during the next year and thus improve our CRS?

SETTING THRESHOLDS

Let's assume a bank has been fined last year, or during the current calendar year, for its involvement in a market abuse.[1] How can we assign one of the four index values [4; 1] displayed in **Figure 23** to this conduct risk marker?

First, a threshold must be associated with a specific level of the four-level scale. This is not a big deal since we work with historical data. We thus know the amount of the fine the bank paid. If not (forecasting approach), it is

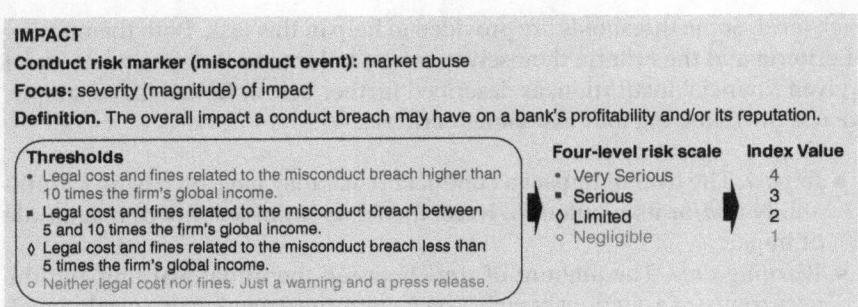

IMPACT

Conduct risk marker (misconduct event): market abuse

Focus: severity (magnitude) of impact

Definition. The overall impact a conduct breach may have on a bank's profitability and/or its reputation.

Thresholds	Four-level risk scale	Index Value
• Legal cost and fines related to the misconduct breach higher than 10 times the firm's global income.	• Very Serious	4
▪ Legal cost and fines related to the misconduct breach between 5 and 10 times the firm's global income.	▪ Serious	3
◊ Legal cost and fines related to the misconduct breach less than 5 times the firm's global income.	◊ Limited	2
○ Neither legal cost nor fines. Just a warning and a press release.	○ Negligible	1

FIGURE 23   From thresholds to index value

required to estimate how much the bank would be fined in case of occurrence of a market abuse. Here is the salient difference between calculating a CRS with historical or estimated data.

Let's assume the fine amount paid by the bank is between 5 and 10 times its global income (the second threshold, indicated by the symbol ▪ in **Figure 23**). The corresponding level in the four-level risk scale is "Serious", which leads to an index value of 3, which, in turn, will result in a high CRS. This is a logical result, since the absolute worst is a CRS of 4 and the absolute best is 1 (see **Figure 22**). Due to a misconduct event (market abuse), this bank experienced a serious drag on its profitability and reputation as well. As a result, the bank faces a high index value, resulting in a high CRS, reflecting poor conduct. This same mechanism applies to the other three assessment criteria in **Figure 24**.

The thresholds related to the warning time criterion are self-explanatory. For example, if a bank can detect a weak signal of market abuse in real time (or almost), meaning a sound conduct risk culture is in place within the bank, its index value will be set at the absolute best of 1. This outstanding index value is explained by the full integration of conduct of business concerns in the bank's governance and conduct risk management arrangements.

Let's take another example of the conduct risk marker—conflicts of interest—related to the conduct risk pillar labelled "Ethics & transparency" in **Figure 22**. If a bank can identify potential conflicts of interest on the trading floor in real time or less than 1 day, it is not purely coincidental. This results from a continuous improvement in conduct risk control, culture and governance. In demonstrating its ability to detect a weak signal of market abuse or conflict of interest, a bank also demonstrates that the board of directors, the risk management department and the compliance function play an important role in conduct risk culture and control. In terms of the CRS, this should be

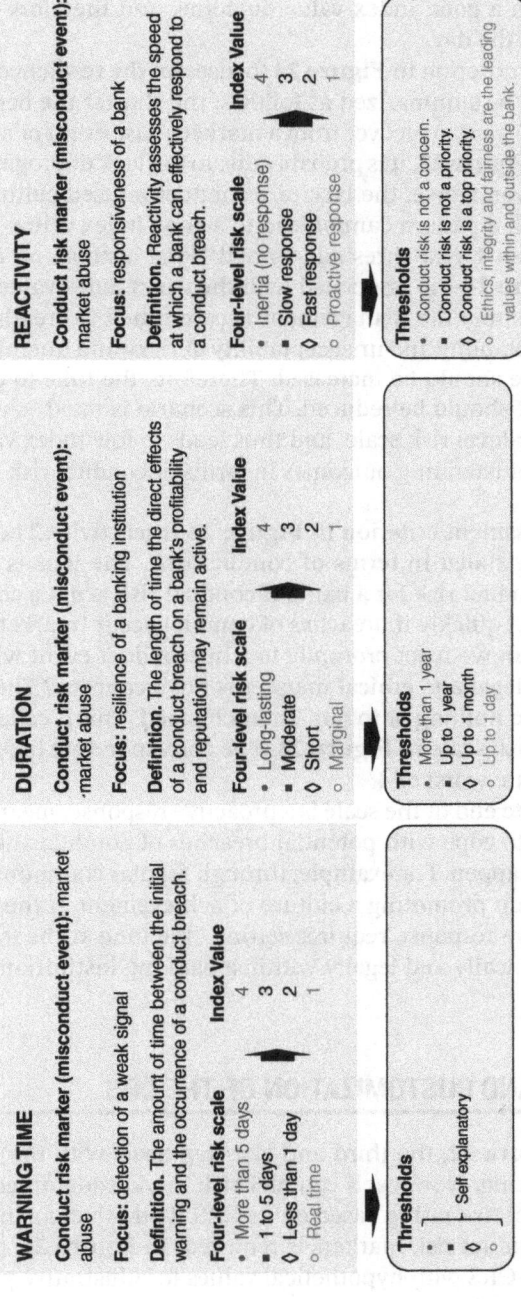

WARNING TIME

Conduct risk marker (misconduct event): market abuse

Focus: detection of a weak signal

Definition. The amount of time between the initial warning and the occurrence of a conduct breach.

Four-level risk scale   **Index Value**
- More than 5 days   4
- 1 to 5 days   3
- ◇ Less than 1 day   2
- ○ Real time   1

Thresholds
- Self explanatory
- ◇
- ○

DURATION

Conduct risk marker (misconduct event): market abuse

Focus: resilience of a banking institution

Definition. The length of time the direct effects of a conduct breach on a bank's profitability and reputation may remain active.

Four-level risk scale   **Index Value**
- Long-lasting   4
- Moderate   3
- ◇ Short   2
- ○ Marginal   1

Thresholds
- More than 1 year
- Up to 1 year
- ◇ Up to 1 month
- ○ Up to 1 day

REACTIVITY

Conduct risk marker (misconduct event): market abuse

Focus: responsiveness of a bank

Definition. Reactivity assesses the speed at which a bank can effectively respond to a conduct breach.

Four-level risk scale   **Index Value**
- Inertia (no response)   4
- Slow response   3
- ◇ Fast response   2
- ○ Proactive response   1

Thresholds
- Conduct risk is not a concern.
- Conduct risk is not a priority.
- ◇ Conduct risk is a top priority.
- ○ Ethics, integrity and fairness are the leading values within and outside the bank.

FIGURE 24 Other examples of thresholds

rewarded through a good index value outcome, and therefore a low (good) CRS at the end of the day.

The duration criterion in **Figure 24** focuses on the resilience of a banking institution. It can be summarized as follows: the shorter the better. If a bank needs more than 1 year to recover from a market abuse event or any other conduct breaches in **Figure 22**, it is probably due to the lack of progress at improving conduct or, even worse, the lack of a conduct-infused culture within the organization. Such a pattern cannot lead to a good index value. This explains why the more-than-1-year threshold—rated "long-lasting" on the four-level risk scale in **Figure 24**—is associated with the worst index value of 4.

In contrast, where the management is committed to creating the conditions for the acceptability and unacceptability of risky and unethical practices, a bank's resilience should be increased. Therefore, the time to get through a misconduct event should be reduced. This scenario is rated "short" or "marginal" on the four-level risk scale, and thus leads to low index values indicating very good to outstanding outcomes in terms of conduct risk management in **Figure 24**.

The last assessment criterion in **Figure 24** is reactivity. The four thresholds are explicitly stated in terms of conduct risk. The idea is to assess the importance of conduct risk for a bank. If conduct risk is not a concern, it will be difficult to react quickly if breaches of conduct occur (market abuse in our example). How can we react promptly to a misconduct event when conducting business in a legal and ethical manner is not a concern? The natural tendency will be to do nothing or to remain unchanged. This is called inertia, the first level in the risk scale in **Figure 24**. The corresponding index value is, of course, the absolute worst of 4.

At the opposite end of the scale is a proactive response, meaning the bank has taken action to cope with potential breaches of conduct and doesn't just react when they happen. For example, through regular communications from senior management promoting a culture of achievement of the conduct outcomes. A proactive response requires setting "the tone at the top" for acting professionally, ethically and legally within a banking institution or any other organization.

CALCULATION AND CUSTOMIZATION OF THE CRS

As shown in **Figure 22**, the third and last step deals with the CRS calculation strictly speaking. Now, each conduct risk marker identified in Step 1 is assigned a conduct risk rating based on its CRS. To do that, an index value for each of the 12 conduct risk markers is required. In **Figure 25**, we derive the calculation of the CRS with hypothetical values for illustrative purposes.

RISK PILLARS	CONDUCT RISK MARKERS	Index Value							
		IMPACT	Mean	WARNING TIME	Mean	DURATION	Mean	REACTIVITY	Mean
Ethics & transparency	• Tax evasion and money laundering	4		3		4		4	
	• Conflicts of interest	4	3.7	3	3.0	4	4.0	4	4.0
	• Unauthorized disclosure of confidential information	3		3		4		4	
Market integrity	• Market abuse	4		4		4		4	
	• Embargo violation	3	3.3	3	3.3	4	4.0	4	4.0
	• Anti-competitive practices	3		3		4		4	
Customers	• Practices contrary to the interest of clients	3		4		3		3	
	• Customers' exposure to an unreported risk	3	3.0	4	3.7	1	1.7	3	3.0
	• Lack of customers' data protection	3		3		1		3	
Fairness	• Gender, racial or religious discrimination	2		2		4		4	
	• Pressure on employees	3	2.3	3	3.0	3	3.7	4	4.0
	• No whistleblower protection	2		3		4		4	

MEAN (3.1) (3.3) (3.3) (3.8)

$$\text{Conduct Risk Score (CRS)} = \frac{3.1 + 3.3 + 3.3 + 3.8}{4} = 3.4$$

FIGURE 25 The mechanics of the CRS

As indicated in **Figure 25**, the CRS is nothing more than a mean of means. The CRS of 3.4 is the mean of the four means obtained by the banking institutions on each index value: (i) impact; (ii) warning time; (iii) duration; and (iv) reactivity. This bank's conduct risk performance is summarized in **Figure 26**. A CRS of 3.4—pretty close to the absolute worst of 4.0—corresponds to a "high-risk" conduct risk rating. This bank is sending clear messages of poor standards of behaviour, failures of operational control, regulatory breaches and illegal activity. In short, poor conduct and misbehaviour.

The above CRS is said to be equally weighted since all index values are weighted in the same way. The underlying assumption is that each index value (impact, waiting time, duration, reactivity) has the same importance in the CRS calculation; they account for 25% each. In other words, they will impact the CRS result with the same strength. This assumption is obviously

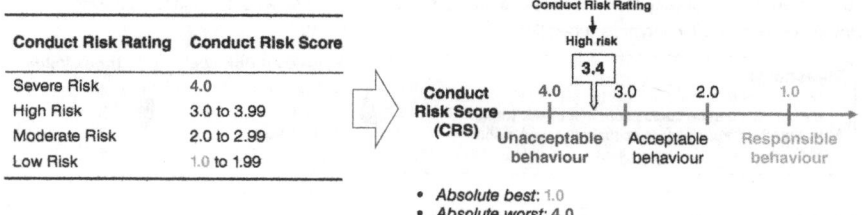

Conduct Risk Rating	Conduct Risk Score
Severe Risk	4.0
High Risk	3.0 to 3.99
Moderate Risk	2.0 to 2.99
Low Risk	1.0 to 1.99

FIGURE 26 Interpreting a CRS

questionable and, therefore, an equally weighted CRS may be used as a baseline scenario. It is possible to weight each index value in **Figure 25** according to their importance, but at the cost of introducing greater subjectivity into the CRS calculation. Defining a weighting scheme is not an easy task. Assuming the following weights: impact (10%), warning time (20%), duration (30%), reactivity (40%), the weighted CRS is calculated as follows (data from **Figure 25**):

$$\text{Weighted CRS} = \left(\boxed{3.1} \times 10\%\right) + \left(\boxed{3.3} \times 20\%\right) + \left(\boxed{3.3} \times 30\%\right) + \left(\boxed{3.8} \times 40\%\right) = 3.5$$

$$\qquad\quad\;\text{IMPACT}\qquad\;\;\text{WARNING}\qquad\text{DURATION}\qquad\text{REACTIVITY}$$
$$\qquad\qquad\qquad\qquad\text{TIME}$$

   The CRS is slightly modified from 3.4 to 3.5. Of course, a weighted CRS can increase or decrease depending on the weighting scheme adopted. This is the main shortfall of a weighted CRS: it could easily be manipulated by financial institutions to disclose good conduct and behaviour. A kind of window-dressing applied to conduct risk. As observed by EY's Patricia Jackson: "*conduct will not improve unless the culture changes too*".[2] A CRS, weighted or not, may help banks understand and improve their risk culture and go down the ethics and conduct route.

   Another way to customize this first example of the CRS is to add another index value into its calculation, or substitute some of the four index values with new ones. It is, of course, still possible to replace all of them with alternative versions. For example, to make the CRS a little bit more predictive, in the hope that this will stimulate a one-step-ahead approach to conduct risk, we might include an index value assessing the probability of occurrence of a conduct risk marker or event (**Figure 27**).

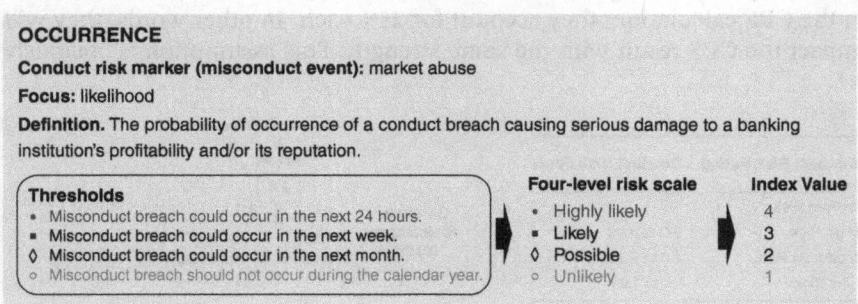

OCCURRENCE

Conduct risk marker (misconduct event): market abuse

Focus: likelihood

Definition. The probability of occurrence of a conduct breach causing serious damage to a banking institution's profitability and/or its reputation.

Thresholds	Four-level risk scale	Index Value
• Misconduct breach could occur in the next 24 hours.	• Highly likely	4
▪ Misconduct breach could occur in the next week.	▪ Likely	3
◊ Misconduct breach could occur in the next month.	◊ Possible	2
○ Misconduct breach should not occur during the calendar year.	○ Unlikely	1

FIGURE 27   A slight customization of the CRS

NOTES

1. Behaviour such as insider trading and market manipulation can amount to market abuse. More generally speaking, a market abuse occurs each time there is an attempt to collude and manipulate prices. That includes the costs of retail banking services, asset prices or benchmark rates.
2. From regulation to results: Bank strategy. *The Banker*, Special Report, January 2015, p. 9.

## CHAPTER 17

Fostering a Culture of Appropriate Conduct Outcomes

CONDUCT RISK CULTURE AND BEHAVIOURS

Do banks really know whether their culture is effective in reducing misconduct? The answer is probably not. Even when banks gather and store behavioural data, they don't know how to make meaningful use of it. It must be acknowledged, however, that culture is not an easily definable concept. The Financial Conduct Authority (FCA) defines culture quite simply as *"the habitual behaviours and mindsets that characterize an organization"*. It is for firms to identify the drivers of behaviour within the firm and control the risks that these drivers create.

As a regulator, the FCA focuses on four key drivers:[1]

■ Purpose
■ Leadership
■ Approach to rewarding and managing people
■ Governance

The idea behind this is to determine how effective each of these drivers of behaviour are in reducing the potential harm in firms.[2] This is not an easy task because each firm's culture is different. There is no one-size-fits-all culture. Our aim here is not to prescribe or promote what an ideal conduct risk culture should be, nor do we believe that every firm should have the same culture. Each firm is responsible for building and maintaining a culture that works in the long-term interests of itself, its customers and market integrity. It is the responsibility of everyone in the banking industry to promote and deliver healthy cultures to prevent harm caused by inappropriate behaviours.

In his speech at the HKMA Annual Conference, Andrew Bailey, initiated a debate on the meaning of culture.[3] Central to this debate is to ask whether culture is an input to institutional behaviour, or is it a summary outcome? According to him: *"there is a distinctive and external 'thing' called culture that acts as an input to institutional behaviour".* Bailey adds that *"there is an important normative part to what is good culture, including good behaviours".*

The challenging question asked by Andrew Bailey, CEO of the FCA (2016–2020), is still pending and the debate still active. When he says that culture is everywhere and nowhere in financial institutions, that's not a big help. Almost everything that goes on in an organization—be it a financial institution or whatever else—affects its culture. No doubt culture in firms is an outcome of many inputs and is characterized by a pattern of behaviours. Where culture is ignored, an opportunity is lost to tackle a key cause of major conduct failings. A conduct risk culture in financial institutions should be a priority. Why? Simply because it is good both for consumers and for markets, thereby reducing the potential for harm.

In what follows, we develop a data-driven approach to cultural change. A key part of this approach is a conduct risk index, explaining how to define, codify and measure conduct risk for individual risk-takers, groups like trading desks in the front office and financial institutions. The aim is to provide banks with a methodology for improving their conduct risk culture by better understanding the root causes of misconduct and acting on them.

It should be acknowledged that culture change in organizations is a challenge, and it may take time because culture can be resilient in the face of attempts to change it. Moreover, it is unrealistic to cover every conduct risk situation—grey areas requiring judgement are unavoidable. However, building a conduct risk index—based on good/expected and bad/unacceptable behaviours—should help banks to drive change and foster their conduct risk culture.

CLARIFYING GOOD AND BAD BEHAVIOURS

The conduct risk index developed here is grounded on three conduct risk pillars: (1) integrity; (2) transparency; and (3) judgement (**Table 29**). They are tailored to reflect expected behaviours from risk-takers or any staff member in a financial institution at the cost of a slight customization. Each pillar is defined from a generic expected behaviour. For example, a trader in a banking institution will demonstrate integrity when he/she *makes sure role mandates are exercised responsibly and legally.* Those three conduct risk pillars are then broken down into five bad/good behaviours. In **Table 29**, they are called negative/positive conduct markers and denoted CM⁻/CM⁺, respectively.

As mentioned before, selecting appropriate pillars and markers is ultimately subjective. The selection displayed in **Table 29** relies mainly on the author's consulting experience in some major banking groups, but also on intuition and common sense. To reduce inherent subjectivity and increase the reliability of the definition of expected behaviours (good and bad), an option is to work closely with the Executive Committee (ExCo) members to set out this list. The first step is to establish a long list from one-on-one interviews with all ExCo members and then to consolidate and align with the banking institution's culture and values in a 1-day workshop focused on conduct. The HR department should also be involved to ensure that existing processes and material are leveraged rather than creating a brand new process or cultural standards. The aim is to develop an operating model workable in a business-as-usual environment.

TABLE 29 Conduct risk markers

CONDUCT RISK PILLAR

① **INTEGRITY**
Makes sure role mandates are exercised responsibly and legally

Negative conduct markers (CM⁻)	Positive conduct markers (CM⁺)
1. Deliberately misprice a product to maximize short-term P&L.	1. Spot abnormal volumes or numbers of deals vs. client context or market conditions.
2. Purposely report wrong prices to clients.	2. Be available for sales and client matters.
3. Access systems or locations that are not reasonably related to one's own responsibilities.	3. Escalate any concerns about potential reputation risks.
4. Promote products not complying with regulation.	4. Evaluate project value and KPI[a] to follow it before launching.
5. Handle new products without prior compliance.	5. Execute the transactions as they have been approved.

② **TRANSPARENCY**
Guarantees reliability of results and operations

Negative conduct markers (CM⁻)	Positive conduct markers (CM⁺)
6. Hide results and positions, whatever the reason.	6. Alert New Products Committee on new products or issues with backlog.
7. Hide known risk issues related to a client to get the transaction approved.	7. Instance NPC[b] when needed, even when not requested by BL.[c]
8. Hide potential conflicts between two clients.	8. Respect suitability guidelines.
9. Hide risk issues from coverage banker[d] to facilitate the sale.	9. Monitor risks on a day-to-day basis.
10. Provide inaccurate transaction information or documents.	10. Record on its books accurately every business transaction.

(*continued*)

TABLE 29 (continued)

③ JUDGEMENT	
Fosters decisions predicated on understanding, analysis and insight	

Negative conduct markers (CM⁻)	Positive conduct markers (CM⁺)
11. Enter into deals putting the bank's reputation at risk.	11. Call attention to existing or potential conflicts of interest (clients/internal).
12. Take any action exceeding one's own mandate.	12. Implement all regulations on KYC,[e] anti-money laundering, market abuse.
13. Provide a client with inappropriate products or services.	13. Develop a strategic view on client needs with the help of the coverage banker.
14. Accept superficial and unsatisfactory explanations in front of an issue.	14. Keep freedom to ask tricky questions and go beyond the obvious.
15. Avoid announcing bad news.	15. Arbitrate business lines when necessary and early enough in the process.

[a]KPI: Key Performance Indicators
[b]NPC: National Payments Council
[c]BL: Bill of Lading (a legal document to make shipping more secure)
[d]Coverage bankers serve as intermediaries between the client and the various departments of the bank. They are the client's main contact. *Source*: Adapted from https://wholesale.banking.societegenerale.com/en/news-insights/glossary.
[e]KYC: Know Your Customer (central to the fight against financial crime and money laundering)

Other pillars and markers can obviously be substituted for those reported, or added to the list. For example, it might be relevant to identify "*don't pay attention to the magnitude of the exposure*" as a bad behaviour related to the last pillar: judgement. However, it requires determining a relevant good/positive counterpart. That could be "*complies with the risk limits trading set by the risk management team*". Anyway, it is always possible to customize the conduct risk pillars and markers as priorities change.

Both bad and good behaviours (negative and positive conduct markers in **Table 29**) are included in the conduct risk index calculation. The rationale is that people displaying some good behaviour can also display bad behaviour—even if they are less likely to misbehave. Considering good behaviour allows staff members acting ethically and legally to be rewarded. The number of good and bad conduct markers in **Table 29** is set arbitrarily to five for each conduct risk pillar. The underlying logic is not to overweight a particular pillar. Integrity, transparency and judgement are equally important in assessing the conduct performance of organizational employees.

MEASURING HOW FAR A RISK-TAKER IS FROM GOOD CONDUCT

Central to the conduct risk index is the distance-to-threshold methodology. The core idea is to define a range of conduct performance with reference to specific low and high conduct performance benchmarks.[4] The lowest-performing individual within the organization establishes the poor conduct performance benchmark (equivalent to 0 on a 0–100 scaled score) and the top-performance benchmark is the threshold or target everyone should reach, ideally speaking (equivalent to 100). Each risk-taker's conduct performance on any conduct risk marker reported in **Table 29** is assessed on a 0–100 scaled score, based on his position within a range defined by the poor and top conduct performance benchmarks, as explained in **Figure 28**.

In the conduct risk index, such as defined in **Figure 28**, achieving or exceeding the threshold is equivalent to a score of 100 on a 0–100 scale. The distance-to-threshold is calculated in absolute terms because a negative distance doesn't make sense, nor would a negative conduct risk index. To compute the 0–100 score of a risk-taker on each conduct risk marker, we gather his/her yearly "Actuals"—the number of misconduct occurrences historically observed.

Although the conduct risk index is primarily developed at the individual level, it can easily be customized at different scales, such as a trading desk (e.g., forex, fixed income, commodities or equities markets), a specific group (e.g., sales vs. traders) or at the bank level. Similarly, the conduct risk index framework and methodology can be applied to shorter or longer time horizons than a year.

Interpreting a conduct risk index value is straightforward. The further away a risk-taker is from the threshold, the higher the distance-to-threshold and thus the lower his/her 0–100 score. Conversely, the closer the risk-taker is to the threshold, the smaller his/her distance-to-threshold and the higher the score. In short, the conduct performance decreases/increases as the 0–100 score gets closer to 0/100, with 0 being the farthest from the threshold (worst

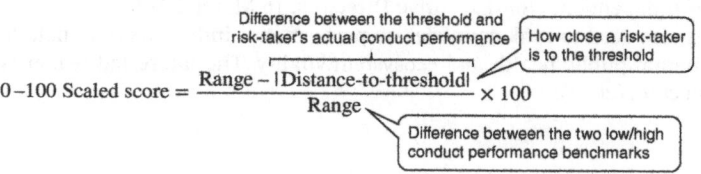

FIGURE 28 The distance-to-threshold method

possible value) and 100 being closest to the threshold (best possible value). The cut-off point between better and worse conduct performance is set arbitrarily to 50. A scaled score of 50 indicates a risk-taker halfway there, meaning he/she is neither a good nor a bad conduct performer.

Selecting appropriate thresholds is subjective per se and depends on the context of the index's objectives. From a conduct risk perspective, zero occurrences of misconduct should be the threshold establishing the top performance benchmark, that is the upper bound of the indicator range in the 0–100 scaled score above. However, a target of zero misconduct is probably too demanding and unrealistic. A group of experts might determine what this high-conduct performance benchmark should be. For example, some members of the middle office in a bank, or a specific committee mixing internal and external skills and competencies.

Along with the top-performance benchmark, it is also required to determine the low end of the indicator range, that is the poor-performance benchmark. This relies heavily on the maximum occurrences of misconduct a financial institution is willing to tolerate. There is no golden rule for this purpose. Typically, the worst-performing entity establishes the low-performance benchmark for a conduct risk marker. Another option is to set this benchmark through peer analysis, that is an impactful apples-to-apples comparison for a similar group of people, such as risk-takers operating in the front office of banks. It can help to identify trends and anomalies in behaviour by averaging the number of misconduct occurrences, but also the dispersion in misbehaviour. Over time, a group of people—be they risk-takers or not—inevitably deviates from what is expected of them. In other words, the average number of misconducts increases and a group's collective understanding of what is tolerable behaviour changes accordingly.

NOTES

1. Source: https://www.fca.org.uk/firms/culture-and-governance
2. We use the term "firm" in a generic way and because this is the term employed by the FCA.
3. Speech by Andrew Bailey, Chief Executive Officer of the FCA, at the HKMA Annual Conference for Independent Non-Executive Directors, 16 March 2017.
4. This method is also used to rank countries on performance indicators that include both environmental public health and ecosystem vitality. The interested reader is referred to Hsu *et al.* (2013).

## CHAPTER 18

Worked Example 8: Calculating a Risk-Taker's Conduct Risk Index

OVERVIEW

It is recommended to compute a risk-taker's conduct risk index step by step. The conduct risk index framework derived from **Table 29** is represented in **Figure 29**. Each conduct risk pillar (integrity, transparency, judgement) is divided into positive and negative conduct risk markers, corresponding to good and bad behaviours, respectively. They appear in **Figure 29** as CM⁻ and CM⁺.

The next steps deal with the calculation of 0–100 scaled scores. First, we compute a score for each positive and negative conduct risk marker. We thus obtain a total of 30 scores (the Score columns in **Figure 29**). These 30 scores are then aggregated at the conduct risk pillar level, which results in six new scores (Aggregated score (0-100)_Geometric in **Figure 29**). From these six scores, we compute an overall score for the negative conduct risk markers and its counterpart for the positive ones. Finally, these two scores are averaged to get the risk-taker conduct risk index. This step-by-step process is summarized in **Figure 30**. The previous score calculations can be performed with a basic Excel spreadsheet without using VBA.[1]

Going back to **Figure 29**, let's have a look at the data displayed and required to implement the step-by-step process described in **Figure 30**. Displayed vertically in **Figure 29** are:

- Low perf. B/High perf. B = poor and top conduct performance benchmarks. As a reminder, both are used to compute the range in **Figure 28**.
- Actuals = number of occurrences historically observed over the past year for a given risk-taker within the banking institution.
- Worst peer perf. = the worst peer conduct performance.
- Range = the difference between the two conduct performance benchmarks (low and high perf. B above).
- Score is the 0–100 scaled score calculated for each negative and positive conduct marker (CM⁻ and CM⁺) matched with each conduct risk pillar.

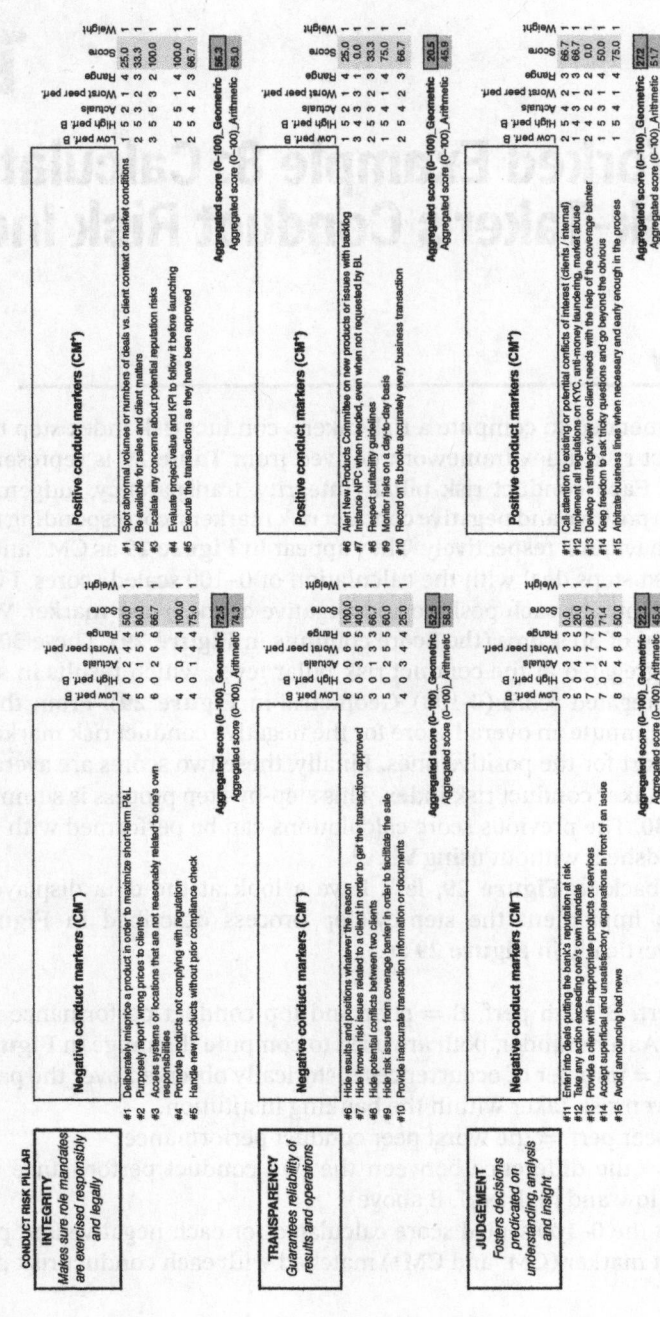

FIGURE 29 The conduct risk index framework

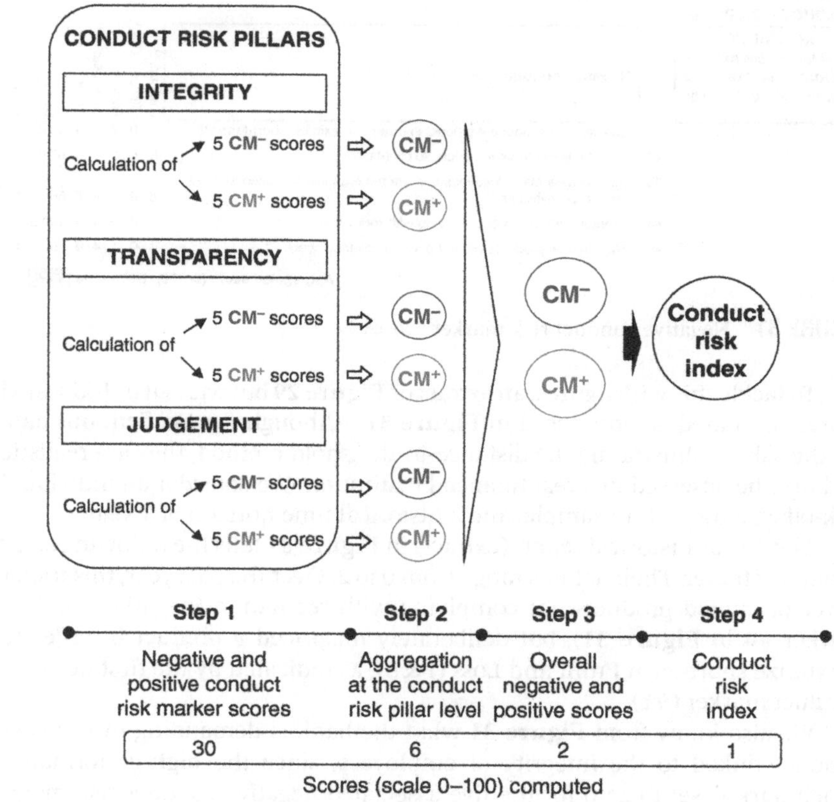

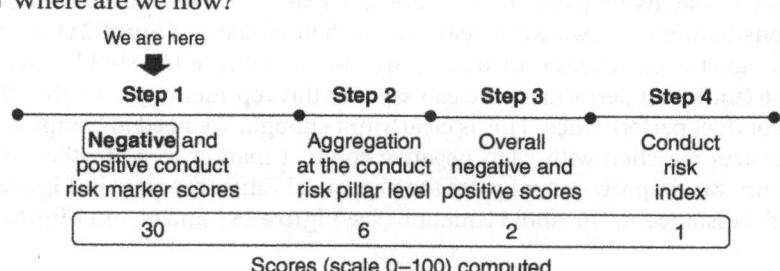

FIGURE 30 Step-by-step process of the conduct risk index

■ Weight, equal to 1 everywhere, indicates that each conduct risk marker is equally important in the score and thus in the aggregated score (0–100). These scores are said to be equally weighted.

CALCULATION OF A NEGATIVE CONDUCT RISK MARKER SCORE

■ Where are we now?

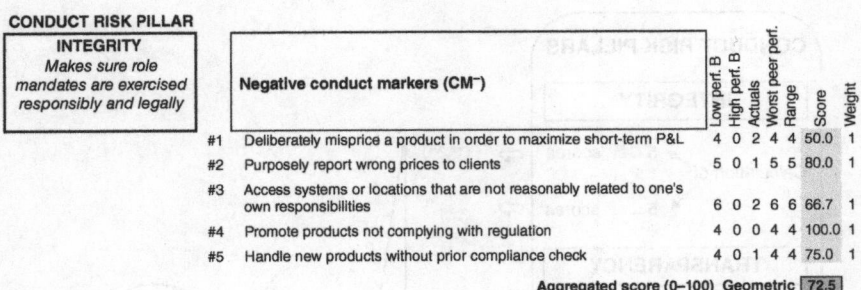

FIGURE 31 Negative conduct risk marker scores

To tackle this with figures, an extract of **Figure 29** but with all 0–100 scaled scores computed is reproduced in **Figure 31**. Although we use fictitious data for the sake of illustrating the distance-to-threshold method, they are realistic and may be observed in a real financial institution. We consider an individual risk-taker, a trader for example, and a historical time horizon of 1 year.

The 1-year historical report (extract) in **Figure 31** tells the following story about our trader. Their actuals range from 0 to 2. Over the past year, this trader never promoted products not complying with regulation (negative conduct marker #4 in **Figure 31**), but deliberately mispriced a product in order to maximize short-term Profit and Loss (P&L), as indicated by the first negative conduct marker (#1).

We also know from **Figure 31** what the bank is demanding in terms of conduct linked to the integrity of employees, since the high-performance benchmark is set to zero for the five associated negative conduct risk markers. This is the threshold each risk-taker in this bank should reach, ideally speaking. In other words, no misconduct occurrences are allowed to be identified as a top conduct performer in terms of integrity in this bank. The low-performance benchmark, indicating poor conduct performance, has been determined by peer analysis and thus corresponds to the worst peer performance in **Figure 31**.

By simply using these data, we can draw a rough conclusion about our trader's conduct performance. For example, focusing on the third negative conduct risk marker (#3 in **Figure 31**), the high-performance benchmark or threshold is 0 and the low/poor-performance benchmark is 6. Our trader accessed systems or locations that are not reasonably related to their own responsibilities only twice last year (this is their actual in **Figure 31**). As two misconduct occurrences (our trader) are closer to 0 (the threshold to reach) than 6 (the worst performer), we can say that this represents good rather than bad conduct performance. This is clearly not enough. We need to compute the five scores matched with each negative conduct marker to go further. With this aim, we simply copy and paste the numerical values reported in **Figure 31** into the distance-to-threshold equation (see **Figure 28**), and obtain **Figure 32**.

$$0\text{--}100 \text{ Scaled score} = \frac{\overbrace{\text{Range} - |\text{Distance-to-threshold}|}^{|\text{Threshold} - \text{Actual}| = |0 - 2| = \mathbf{2}} \boxed{\text{Proximity-to-threshold}}}{\text{range}} \times 100$$

Range of conduct performance with reference to specific high- and low-performance benchmarks

Low − high perf. B = 6 − 0 = **6**

$$0\text{--}100 \text{ Scaled score} = \frac{6-2}{6} \times 100 = 66.7$$

FIGURE 32   Example of a 0–100 scaled score calculation

The score of our trader on the third negative conduct marker "*Access systems or locations that are not reasonably related to one's own responsibilities*", linked with the first conduct risk pillar "Integrity" in **Figure 31**, is equal to 66.7. This score reflects our previous rough conclusion drawn without any calculation. Our trader's conduct performance on this specific conduct marker is not so bad. Not outstanding, but there is nothing shameful about this score either. This pretty good conduct performance is due to our trader's proximity-to-threshold. With an actual equal to 2, their position within the range established by the lowest-performing risk-taker (6) and the threshold (0) is closer to the latter than the former. The other scores in **Figure 31** are calculated following the same method as for the negative conduct marker #3 displayed in **Figure 32**.

- Negative conduct marker #1

$$0\text{--}100 \text{ scaled score} = \frac{4-2}{4} \times 100 = 50.0$$

- Negative conduct marker #2

$$0\text{--}100 \text{ scaled score} = \frac{5-1}{5} \times 100 = 80.0$$

- Negative conduct marker #3

   See **Figure 32**.

- Negative conduct marker #4

$$0\text{--}100 \text{ scaled score} = \frac{4-0}{4} \times 100 = 100$$

- Negative conduct marker #5

$$0\text{--}100 \text{ scaled score} = \frac{4-1}{4} \times 100 = 75$$

SCORES AGGREGATION AND FULL OFFSETTING

- Where are we now?

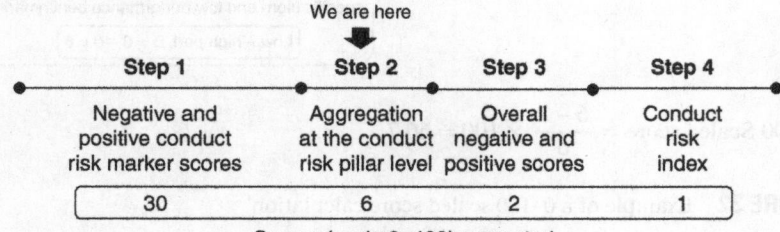

Scores (scale 0–100) computed

To compute the aggregated 0–100 scaled score that sums up the conduct performance of our trader in terms of integrity, based on their scores obtained on each negative conduct marker #1 to #5, different aggregation methods are available.

The most widespread and simplest method is the arithmetic mean or linear aggregation. Averaging the five negative conduct marker scaled scores leads to the following aggregated score (0–100):

$$\text{Aggregated score (0–100)} = \frac{50.0 + 80.0 + 66.7 + 100 + 75}{5} \times 100 = 74.3$$

An undesirable feature of linear aggregation is the full offsetting it implies. To put it simply, a low performance in some conduct markers can be compensated by a higher performance in other conduct markers. This is due to the fact that the linear aggregation method is by essence additive. In the above arithmetic mean, we add the five scores to obtain the aggregated score (0–100). To alleviate this shortcoming, we use a geometric aggregation method instead. This method is multiplicative and does not allow for full offsetting between conduct markers.

As shown in **Figure 31**, the aggregated score (0–100) for the five negative conduct markers matched with the first conduct risk pillar "Integrity" is equal to 72.5. This score is the geometric mean of the five scores obtained for the negative conduct markers. We use the Excel statistical function GEOMEAN. This function returns the geometric mean. We thus have the following two aggregated scores (0–100):

- Geometric mean: 72.5
- Arithmetic mean: 74.3

This is a very good conduct performance in terms of integrity, regardless of which mean is used. The difference between the two means is small but could be significant, see the third conduct risk pillar "Judgement" in **Figure 29**. We obtain 22.2 (geometric) vs. 45.4 (arithmetic).

Readers not familiar with Excel functions can compute the geometric mean without using the function GEOMEAN. The geometric mean is defined as the nth root of the product of n numbers. Formally, it is expressed as follows:

$$\text{Geometric mean} = \left(\prod_{i=1}^{n} x_i\right)^{i/n} = \sqrt[n]{x_1 \times x_2 \ldots \times x_n}$$

The $\prod$ symbol is the mathematical notation for "product", like the Σ in summation notation

The nth root of the product of n numbers

This formula says to multiply items together and then to take the nth root – where n is the number of items.[2] While the arithmetic mean adds numbers, the geometric mean multiplies numbers. This explains why the linear aggregation method (arithmetic mean) is said to be additive, and the geometric aggregation method (geometric mean) is said to be multiplicative. Using the five scores in **Figure 31**, we have

$$\text{Geometric mean} = (50.0 \times 80.0 \times 66.7 \times 100.0 \times 75.0)^{1/5} = 72.5$$

To illustrate further why the geometric mean does not allow for full offsetting, and might thus be more appealing than the arithmetic mean from a risk management viewpoint, let's take the toy example of a bank with only two traders X and Y. Their scores (0–100) on four hypothetical conduct markers are reported in **Table 30**.

The two traders obtain the same aggregated 0–100 scaled scores, equal to 32.75, when calculated with the linear aggregation method (arithmetic mean). Yet they display substantially different conduct risk profiles, as reported by the conduct markers #1 to #4. This difference is not reflected in their aggregated

TABLE 30 Baseline scenario

Conduct Marker	Trader X	Trader Y
#1	96.8	32.75
#2	11.4	32.75
#3	11.4	32.75
#4	11.4	32.75
Arithmetic mean	32.75	32.75
Geometric mean	19.46	32.75

scores due to the drawback of the linear aggregation method. The geometric aggregation method (geometric mean) generates an aggregated score more in line with what is displayed in **Table 30**. Trader X cannot offset their very bad conduct performance on the conduct markers #2 to #4 with their very good performance on the first marker (96.8). At the end of the day, their aggregated score (19.46) is lower than that of trader Y.

The geometric mean is also appealing because it leads to different incentives for our two traders X and Y. To understand why, let's assume that both traders increase the second conduct marker #2 by 1, 3 and 5 points, meaning an improved conduct performance on this specific marker. What happens? The results of these three scenarios are reported in **Table 31**.

As indicated in **Table 31**, the 1-point increase in conduct marker #2 is more interesting for trader X than Y, since they improve their aggregated score by +2.13%, from 19.46 (the baseline scenario in **Table 30)** to 19.87 (the geometric mean in **Table 31**), against less than 1% for trader Y. It becomes even more attractive for trader X versus Y when the former improves their conduct performance by more than 1 point. An increase by 3 points is converted into a 3.81% increase in their aggregated score (vs. only 1.45% for trader Y). An increase by 5 points leads to a 9.52% increase in trader X's aggregated score and only 3.62% for Y. Clearly, the same x-point marginal increase is not equally rewarded between traders X and Y.

The message conveyed by the geometric aggregation to risk-takers operating in a banking institution is obvious: should you be interested in improving your aggregated score on a given conduct risk pillar, focus on your lowest scores and not only the better ones. From the bank standpoint, aggregating scores (0–100) for different conduct risk pillars through geometric means might motivate risk-takers to focus and improve their conduct weaknesses.

TABLE 31   Three scenarios of an improved conduct performance

	Scenario 1 Increase by 1 point		Scenario 2 Increase by 3 points		Scenario 3 Increase by 5 points	
Conduct Marker	**Trader X**	**Trader Y**	**Trader X**	**Trader Y**	**Trader X**	**Trader Y**
#1	96.8	32.75	96.8	32.75	96.8	32.75
#2	**12.4**	**33.75**	**14.4**	**35.75**	**16.4**	**37.75**
#3	11.4	32.75	11.4	32.75	11.4	32.75
#4	11.4	32.75	11.4	32.75	11.4	32.75
Geometric mean	19.87	33.0	20.63	33.48	21.31	33.93
Increase*	2.13%	0.75%	3.81%	1.45%	9.52%	3.62%

* Against the baseline scenario defined in **Table 30**.

This toy example with two traders shows that there is an incentive for risk-takers to leave their comfort zone. It is more interesting for trader X—the low performer—to improve their conduct performance on the second marker and thus their aggregated score. This can be reinforced through a bonus policy aligned with a conduct risk index upgrade—evaluated on a yearly basis, for example.

POSITIVE CONDUCT RISK MARKER SCORES

- Where are we now?

We are here

Step 1	Step 2	Step 3	Step 4
Negative and [positive] conduct risk marker scores	Aggregation at the conduct risk pillar level	Overall negative and positive scores	Conduct risk index
30	6	2	1

Scores (scale 0–100) computed

We go back to Step 1 but this time to explain how to cope with *positive* (good) conduct marker scores. For the sake of clarity, we reproduce in **Figure 33** an extract of **Figure 29**, where the positive or good conduct markers matched with the first conduct risk pillar ("Integrity") are displayed.

The calculation of scores is like that used for negative or bad conduct markers, but we rely on a 360-degree assessment performed by colleagues against those markers to set both the low and high conduct performance benchmarks. This is achieved through a five-point Likert scale ranging from "strongly disagree" (coded 1) to "strongly agree" (coded 5), as illustrated

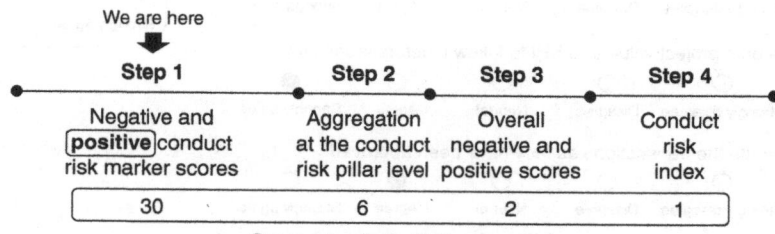

CONDUCT RISK PILLAR

INTEGRITY Makes sure role mandates are exercised responsibly and legally	Positive conduct markers (CM⁺)	Low perf. B	High perf. B	Actuals	Worst peer perf.	Range	Score	Weight
	#1 Spot abnormal volumes or numbers of deals vs. client context or market conditions	1	5	2	1	4	25.0	1
	#2 Be available for sales and client matters	2	5	3	2	3	33.3	1
	#3 Escalate any concerns about potential reputation risks	3	5	5	3	2	100.0	1
	#4 Evaluate project value and KPI to follow it before launching	1	5	5	1	4	100.0	1
	#5 Execute the transactions as they have been approved	2	5	4	2	3	66.7	1

Aggregated score (0–100)_Geometric **56.3**

FIGURE 33 Positive conduct markers (Integrity)

INTEGRITY
Makes sure role mandates are exercised responsibly and legally
Positive conduct markers (CM⁺)

#1 Spot abnormal volumes or numbers of deals vs. client context or market conditions

       ○   ●   ○   ○   ○
   Strongly disagree   Disagree   Neutral   Agree   Strongly agree

#2 Be available for sales and client matters

       ○   ○   ●   ○   ○
   Strongly disagree   Disagree   Neutral   Agree   Strongly agree

#3 Escalate any concerns about potential reputation risks

       ○   ○   ○   ○   ●
   Strongly disagree   Disagree   Neutral   Agree   Strongly agree

#4 Evaluate project value and KPI to follow it before launching

       ○   ○   ○   ○   ●
   Strongly disagree   Disagree   Neutral   Agree   Strongly agree

#5 Execute the transactions as they have been approved

       ○   ○   ○   ●   ○
   Strongly disagree   Disagree   Neutral   Agree   Strongly agree

Coding	
Strongly disagree	1
Disagree	2
Neutral	3
Agree	4
Strongly agree	5

FIGURE 34 Likert scale for positive conduct markers

in **Figure 34**.[3] The range is still established with reference to high and low conduct performance benchmarks, but the definition of both benchmarks is modified. The lowest performance benchmark corresponds to "strongly disagree" on the Likert scale, and the highest to "strongly agree". The former established the weakest conduct performance (coded 1), and the latter defines the target (coded 5).

We select a five-point scale because an odd number provides the respondent with a neutral level when he/she has no opinion on a matter related to a given conduct marker. This neutral position indicates that the respondent neither disagrees nor agrees with the statement under review. In contrast, an even number of points results in a series of forced questions, meaning that respondents are forced to give their opinion. Then, each employee involved in the 360-degree assessment responds to each item via the five-point scale to indicate the extent to which he/she disagrees or agrees.

The example in **Figure 34** reports a hypothetical answer from an employee asked to assess a trader's conduct performance in terms of integrity. It should be noted that this employee can be a peer—a trader operating on the same desk or financial products, for example—but not only that. The scope of 360-degree assessment or feedback is much larger than a peer analysis. In the former, feedback is received from everyone with whom the employee under review has interacted during their daily business operations. This can be peers, subordinates, managers or even external stakeholders such as clients (traders operating in other banks, for example). It is also worth mentioning that when you are involved in a 360-degree assessment, you receive an analysis of how others perceive you but also how you perceive yourself. For each risk-taker, comparison of self-perception against the perceptions of others is thus possible.

Using the coding in **Figure 34**, we obtain the actuals in **Figure 33** for the trader under review:

- Conduct marker #1: "disagree" → coded 2
- Conduct marker #2: "neutral" → coded 3
- Conduct marker #3: "strongly agree" → coded 5
- Conduct marker #4: "strongly agree" → coded 5
- Conduct marker #5: "strongly agree" → coded 4

The series {2, 3, 5, 5, 4} defines the actuals required to compute the five 0–100 scaled scores in **Figure 33** through the distance-to-threshold method—as we did for the negative conduct markers. A lower score indicates a worse conduct performance, and a higher score the opposite. The resulting aggregated score (0–100)—still calculated with a geometric mean—is 56.3. This is an average performance. As a reminder, the aggregated score calculated from the negative or bad conduct markers matched with the same conduct pillar—Integrity—was equal to 72.5. This difference may be explained by both different conduct markers and low/high-performance benchmarks as set out. Although bad and good conduct markers may be considered as two sides of the same coin, they do not convey exactly the same information.

CALCULATION OF THE OVERALL SCORES

- Where are we now?

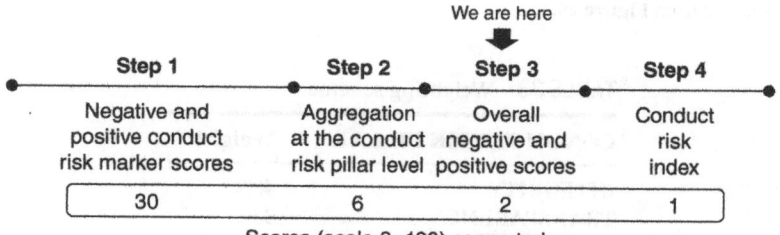

Scores (scale 0–100) computed

The overall negative and positive scores are calculated by averaging (geometric mean) the six aggregated scores (0–100) displayed in **Figure 29**. For the sake of comparison, we also report in **Table 32** the overall scores obtained when using an arithmetic mean.

As explained before, the geometric mean (or aggregation) does not allow for full offsetting. This explains why the overall scores calculated with an arithmetic mean are higher in **Table 32** and will be most flattering in terms of conduct risk.

Another way to proceed is to compute weighted overall scores according to the rule "What matters weighs more". For example, let's consider that integrity is more important than transparency, that is itself more important than judgement. We would then have the weighting scheme in **Table 33**.

The objective here is to transfer the weighting scheme into the overall scores so as to reflect the respective magnitude of each conduct risk pillar. If we consider that integrity overtakes transparency and judgement, that should

TABLE 32 Unweighted overall negative and positive scores

Unweighted	Aggregated Scores (0–100)_Geometric mean*	
CONDUCT RISK PILLAR	Negative Conduct Markers (CM⁻)	Positive Conduct Markers (CM⁺)
INTEGRITY	72.5	56.3
TRANSPARENCY	52.5	20.5
JUDGEMENT	22.2	27.2
Overall score	**43.9**	**31.5**
	Aggregated Scores (0–100)_Arithmetic mean*	
INTEGRITY	74.3	65.0
TRANSPARENCY	58.3	45.9
JUDGEMENT	45.4	51.7
Overall score	**49.1**	**34.7**

* Reproduced from **Figure 29**.

TABLE 33 Weighting scheme

CONDUCT RISK PILLAR	Weight
INTEGRITY	40%
TRANSPARENCY	35%
JUDGEMENT	25%
Total	**100%**

be echoed both in the overall negative and positive scores and therefore in the conduct risk index. Unfortunately, Excel does not provide a statistical function for calculating a weighted geometric mean. Therefore, we must customize the unweighted geometric mean formula used before to insert our weighting scheme. This is done through the formula

$$\text{Weighted geometric mean} = \left(\prod_{i=1}^{n} x_i^{w_i} \right)^{1/\sum_{i=1}^{n} w_i}$$

Aggregated scores (0–100)_Geometric in **Figure 29**

The sum of weights $w_1, w_2, \ldots, w_n$

Weighting scheme in **Table 33**

Indicates that a product is being computed

As an example, we compute below the overall weighted CM⁻ score for the first conduct risk pillar in **Figure 29** ("Integrity"):

$$\text{Weighted geometric mean} = [(72.5)^{0.40} \times (52.5)^{0.35}(22.2)^{0.25}]^{1/(0.40+0.35+0.25)}$$

$$= [48.17]^{1} = 48.17$$

For the sake of clarity, the details of the calculation according to a four-step approach are displayed in **Table 34**. This table is built with the aim of being reproduced in an Excel spreadsheet without difficulty.

In **Table 34**, Step 3 is equal to 1 since the sum of weights equals 1. It should be noted, however, that this does not always hold true and depends on the nature of your weights.

TABLE 34 Calculation of an overall weighted score

CONDUCT RISK PILLAR	Aggregated Score (0–100)_Geometric x_i	Weight w_i	Step 1 $x_i^{w_i}$	Step 2 Products of the Outputs from Step 1	Step 3 $\dfrac{1}{\sum_{i=1}^{3} w_i}$	Step 4 Result
INTEGRITY	72.5	0.40	5.55			
TRANSPARENCY	52.5	0.35	4.00			
JUDGEMENT	22.2	0.25	2.17			
Sum of weights		1.00				
				48.17	1.00	48.17

Note: The Aggregated score (0–100)_Geometric extracted from **Figure 29** and weights from **Table 33**.

As an example, a marketing firm conducts a survey of 20 households to determine the average number of cell phones each household owns.[4] Your x_i are the number of cell phones per household (e.g., 1, 2, 3, 4, 5) and your w_i are the number of households (e.g., 2, 5, 6, 4, 3). Then

$$\frac{1}{\sum_{i=1}^{5} w_i} = \frac{1}{20} = 0.05$$

which is obviously different from 1.

The six negative and positive aggregated scores (0–100) Geometric reported in **Figure 29** are obtained through the four-step method described in **Table 34**. To highlight the difference between unweighted and weighted overall scores, we display both below:

	Weighted	**Unweighted**
Negative overall score (0–100)	48.17	43.89
Positive overall score (0–100)	32.94	31.53

The not so significant difference between weighted and unweighted overall scores is due to the exponent

$$\frac{1}{\sum_{i=1}^{3} w_i}$$

equal to 1 in **Table 34**.

CALCULATION OF THE CONDUCT RISK INDEX

- Where are we now?

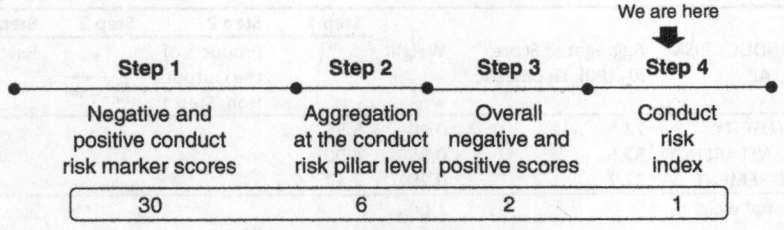

This is the last step, consisting of averaging the negative and positive scores (Step 3) to obtain the final output, that is the 0–100 scaled conduct risk index for the trader under review. We use a simple mean to compute the conduct risk index, as indicated in **Figure 35**.[5]

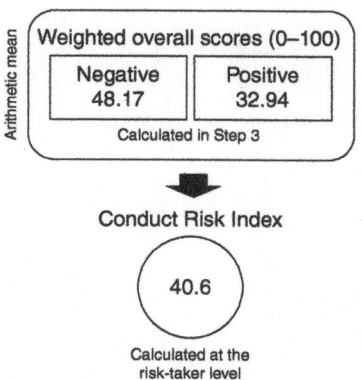

FIGURE 35 Conduct risk index value

The conduct performance of this risk-taker—such as measured through his/her conduct 0–100 scaled risk index—is below average, indicating a poor conduct performance. We remember that an appealing feature of the conduct risk index is to be scalable to a larger unit of analysis (e.g., desk, trading room, strategic unit or the banking institution itself).

NOTES

1. VBA = Visual Basic for Applications. VBA is used to write programmes for the Windows operating system and runs as an internal programming language in Microsoft Office.
2. The geometric mean requires positive numbers. Also worth mentioning, the geometric mean is lower than the arithmetic mean unless all items are equal, in which case the two means are equal.
3. The Likert scale was developed in the early 1930s by the American psychologist Rensis Likert. Initially used in psychological analyses, the Likert rating scale is nowadays widely used in management sciences to measure opinions, attitudes or behaviours.
4. This example comes from Anderson (2013).
5. We use a geometric mean to compute the negative and positive overall scores (0–100) and then a simple (arithmetic) mean to compute the conduct risk index. There is no problem there.

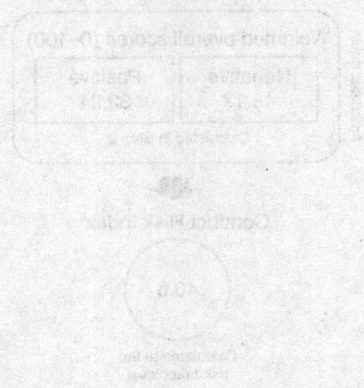

## CHAPTER 19

Hot Questions Still Pending

The conduct risk index developed in this book results from a major study with an investment bank that is attempting a process of this kind. The methodology is grounded on the author's consulting experience, working with strong global players in the banking industry. The conduct risk index has been well received by most risk-takers (mainly, traders and sales) within the banking institution. Specifically, the conduct risk index approach helped them to clarify what was expected of them and identify the key organizational weaknesses that needed to be fixed. It should be said, however, that some hot questions are still pending or only partially solved. In what follows, we list some of them and suggest the beginnings of an answer.[1]

■ *Who is going to carry out the conduct reports/scores? Who is rating whom, how and with what frequency?*

The rating of risk-takers is carried out through a 360-degree performance assessment carried out by the bank's HR department. It is performed by the various persons who are related to the trader and sales in scope (i.e., middle office, compliance function, head of desks, sales working with the trader, legal department, etc.). This 360-degree assessment is performed once a year, but this is only one source of information. Another source comes from the various quarterly and monthly reporting that the bank has in place. This includes front-office supervision, monthly audit reports, monthly/quarterly conduct risk management information, monthly operational risk report, some alerts from the surveillance system (communication and other controls) and any qualitative information received at the ExCo as part of the Senior Manager Report.[2]

■ *How do you juxtapose the conduct risk index against the performance of an employee who is not a Profit and Loss (P&L) centre (i.e., not a trader with his/her own P&L)?*

The current version of the conduct risk index focuses on employees with P&L (mainly, traders and sales). For employees who are not profit centres (without their own P&L), the conduct risk index methodology holds true, but the focus will be on other types of conduct risk markers. Other factors (e.g., leadership and organizational constructs) should be taken on board and embedded in a more qualitative approach.

- *Are individuals anonymized? Who has access rights to the data (right to know, right to act, etc.)?*

Yes, they are. The data are treated as very confidential. The data-gathering and storage follows the existing policy related to personal data and complies with GDPR (General Data Protection Regulation). While reporting comes from different sources and functions, the consolidation and analysis of data is owned by the HR and compliance departments. However, when these data are enriched with personal employee data to better understand the root causes of good and bad behaviours, only HR gets access to it. Compliance and heads of business are given the conduct risk index for employees and the details—not the root cause analysis.

- *Can we envisage some sort of points system, like on a driving licence, that could lead to a ban from practicing as a fund manager, trader or whatever?*

The overall sequence of interrelations works to avoid (or at least mini-mize) the risk of misconduct. The conduct risk index is embedded in the pre-vailing performance appraisal and the compensation system defined by HR. The consistency between the bonus allocated to each risk-taker and his/her conduct risk performance is checked. The aim is not to cap the level of remu-neration or bonuses of risk-takers, but rather to act on its structure and the incentives created. This implies that bonusable employees have knowledge and understand the conduct risk index methodology and its consequences for personal monetary rewards. Communication and induction programmes can be implemented to cascade the conduct risk index philosophy.

The objective here is to reduce the incentives that induce or encourage bad behaviour to preserve bonuses, even in situations where they are very modest. This is where "tone from the top" comes into practice. Top manage-ment's commitment to conduct risk is crucial to risk-taking staff's ethical and legal behaviours. The Board and ExCo members are responsible for setting the value placed on money relative to that of conduct. The tone of the top drives the behaviour of staff and the outcomes they deliver.

As an alternative to a points system like on a driving licence, we consider a percentile analysis of the conduct risk indexes to commensurate individual bonuses with good conduct. As an example, let's assume a trader obtaining a conduct risk index in the 95th percentile. That means he/she scored better than 95% of risk-takers within the organization. Clearly, this trader belongs to the top performers. As a result, his/her bonus (or the part of the bonus directly linked to conduct performance) should be amongst the highest. In contrast, for risk-takers reporting a conduct risk score in the 5th or 10th percentiles (only 5% or 10% of conduct risk indexes in the organization are lower), a penalty could be applied. A more fine-grained bonus/penalty scheme cannot be meaningfully determined without the HR department.

- *How do you prevent a situation arising where the scorer and the scored collude?*

If we look back at one of the most famous misconduct events in recent years—Kerviel's fraud at Société Générale in France—the 360-degree assessment might have reduced its probability of occurrence. As the 360-degree feedback involves a large scope of stakeholders, it turns out that playing the game of "I will scratch your back, if you scratch mine" is practically impossible. The trader Jerome Kerviel colluded with someone operating in the middle office of the French bank. That explains why he managed to hide his huge losses due to rogue trading for such a long time.

- *Are we bad at predicting "bad apples"?*

The conduct risk index developed in this book makes the implicit assumption that the problem of misconduct is about bad apples, that is misbehaving employees identifiable as outliers in an organization. The prevailing organizational theory is that of "bad barrels", whereby risky and unethical behaviours are understood as a product of organizational environments. In other words, "good" people placed in "bad" environments end up doing bad things.[3] Setting too demanding performance goals can foster risky behaviour, leading to misconduct events (e.g., rogue trading) to preserve bonuses and reach performance targets, even if you are not a truly incorrigible bad apple.

Those environments may encompass a "money-priming" culture, where regulators, bonus systems or the frame of reference within which risk-takers make decisions. They contribute to the advent of bad apples in organizations by encouraging them to exploit the weaknesses of a deficient conduct risk management. An illustrative example is breaches of conduct that are tacitly accepted if they lead to good P&L results. Unethical behaviours can become normalized in an organization, and are either seen as necessary and unproblematic, or purely and simply denied, due to the lack of integrity from the leadership (the Board, ExCo, senior management, committees). This explains why integrity is one of the three conduct pillars at the core of the conduct risk index calculation.

What is the conduct risk index developed in this book doing about it? Hopefully, making the deviant behaviour of bad apples easier to identify and more clearly unacceptable; forcing them to either modify their behaviour or exit the organization.

NOTES

1. The author would like to thank Anette Mikes from Saïd Business School, University of Oxford and David Champion, editor of *Harvard Business Review*, for raising these issues.
2. ExCo: Executive Committee (a group of people appointed or elected as the decision-making body of an organization).
3. This is known as the "Stanford Prisoner Experiment" led by Philip Zimbardo, a psychology professor at Stanford University, in 1971. For interested readers, the reference is Zimbardo (2011).

## CHAPTER 20

Understanding the Root Causes of Poor Conduct

In this final chapter, I will draw on my consulting experience with numerous banks to describe what they need to do to detect misconduct early enough to do something about it. The dataset used in what follows was designed and built jointly with an investment bank I advise (as a contractor within a team of consultants), to redesign its process for managing conduct risk.[1]

The dataset records 157 conduct risk indices of traders and sales. As shown in **Figure 36**, most risk-takers lie in the range from 56 to 75, and the lowest conduct performers only represent 4% of the distribution. At first sight, this bank reports quite a sound conduct risk situation. But what about the 25% of those employees who do not behave as expected, or are just above the 50% borderline? What about the impact on the bank's conduct performance? It is difficult to say that it is positive. This is where a more detailed analysis is necessary to better understand the root causes of poor conduct.

CLUSTERING RISK-TAKERS

To get to the bottom of this non-satisfactory conduct performance, we used a cluster methodology to uncover potential hidden realities among employees. Clustering is a method of unsupervised machine learning. Its goal is to partition

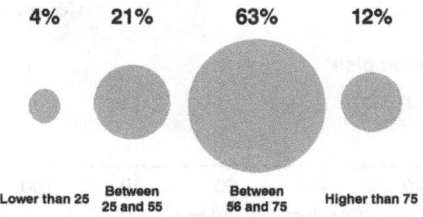

FIGURE 36 The conduct risk index distribution

the observations in a dataset (here, we have 157 risk-takers) into groups or clusters so that the pairwise dissimilarities between those assigned to the same cluster tend to be smaller than those in different clusters.[2] In other words, the aim of clustering is to maximize within-group homogeneity while maximizing between-group heterogeneity.

An appealing feature of cluster analysis is that it is an unsupervised learning, which means that insights are naturally derived from the data without any predefined groups. In an unsupervised setting like clustering, we ignore the partitioning of groups, so we must select the best model to reveal a clustering structure in the data. As we have no ex-ante information about that, we need a tool to identify the number of groups that create clusters where intra-cluster similarity is the highest and inter-cluster similarity is the lowest. Such a tool is called an information criterion. One of the most widely used is the BIC (Bayesian Information Criterion), because it has been shown to be efficient on practical grounds.[3] The rule of thumb is to select the n-group solution yielding the lowest value for the BIC. This indicates the best solution in terms of intra- versus inter-cluster similarity. To give evidence for a four-group structure of the data frame under review here (157 risk-takers), we have used the BIC.[4]

To perform a cluster analysis and generate a companion graph for visualizing outputs, it is also required to define two variables used to plot the groups resulting from the clustering analysis. We select the conduct risk index (x-axis) and the Profit and Loss (P&L) (y-axis) (see **Figure 37**). The interest is in

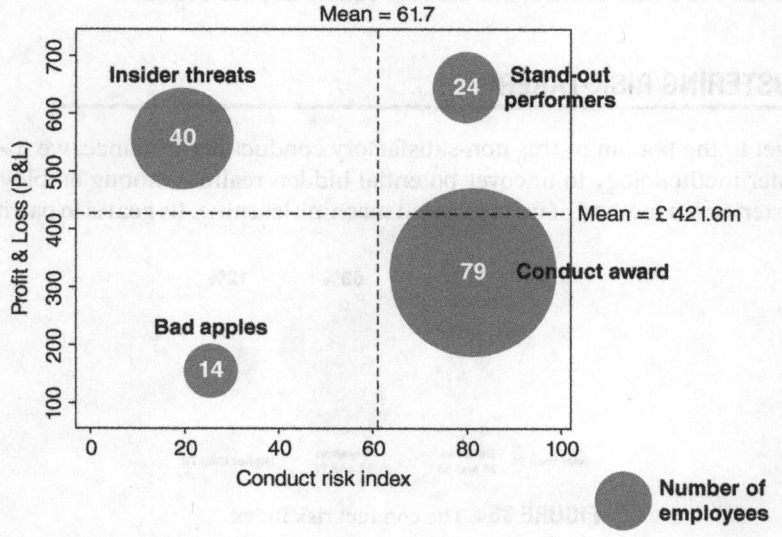

FIGURE 37 The conduct risk matrix

grouping together risk-takers with similar conduct and financial performance into mutually exclusive classes. Then, we can observe whether good conduct is linked with higher financial performance (the 157 risk-takers in our sample are employees with P&L: traders and sales). Do the good people doing the right thing outperform the bad people doing the wrong thing? Answering this question should make sense to a banking institution.

The output from the cluster analysis is given in **Figure 37**. Each cluster identifies a profile of risk-takers, from "stand-out performers" (highest profits generated but still conducting business in a legal and ethical manner), through "conduct award" (highest conduct performance but at the cost of an average or below-average P&L performance), "insider threats" (employees who could potentially put the banking institution at risk) and finally "bad apples" (the truly incorrigible, unethical rule breakers that inevitably crop up in any large organization).

Balancing profit generation with a relatively risk-adverse culture can lead to unsolvable conflicts of interest, where risk-takers are forced to decide between the profit-making interests of management and regulatory adherence. Besides, "*identifying potential conflicts of interest is a tricky issue for banks*", says Will Denis, managing director of compliance at the Association for Financial Markets in Europe.[5] To illustrate, he takes the example of a foreign exchange trader who pre-hedges ahead of a client transaction. This may appear to be in conflict with the client's interest. But how can a trader demonstrate that pre-hedging by the bank is always in the best interests of the client?

Conflicts of interest between following management directives (posting stronger gains) and acting ethically and legally (e.g., in the fair valuation of the underlying assets) can exacerbate misconduct breaches like rogue trading. This explains why the four profiles identified through the conduct risk matrix (**Figure 37**) are not frozen in time. Some risk-takers can evade conduct risk discipline by moving from the "insider threats" to "bad apples" cluster, or the opposite. These migrations within the conduct risk matrix should be closely monitored to prevent potential large fines and losses.

It is paramount for banking institutions to cope with this rolling bad apples phenomenon and prove to regulators, but also internally to organizational employees (those who contribute effectively to the successful functioning of an organization) that they understand and manage conduct risk.[6]

IN-DEPTH ANALYSIS OF BAD APPLES

The most concerning cluster in **Figure 37** is clearly the "bad apples", where employees are weak both in terms of profit generation (low P&L) and conduct performance (low conduct risk index). To investigate the root causes,

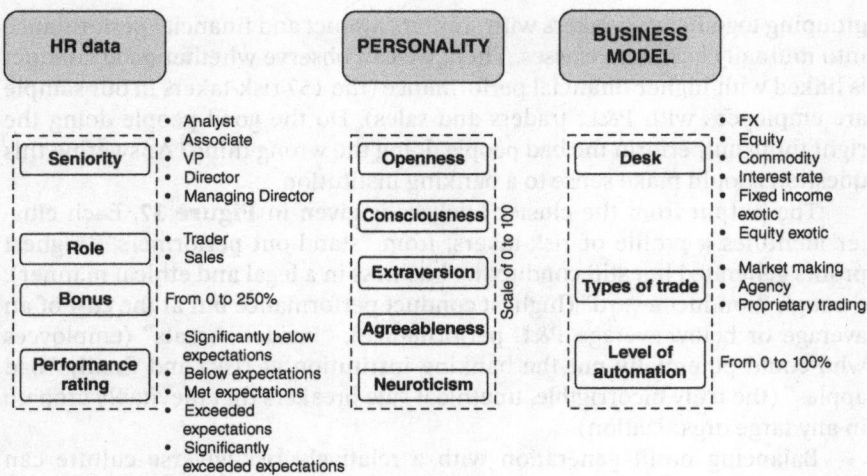

FIGURE 38 Additional factors for explaining conduct risk

we perform a deep-dive analysis. The idea is to enrich the conduct risk index framework with other factors than P&L and the conduct risk index. These additional factors, displayed in **Figure 38**, are supposed to impact directly or indirectly on the conduct performance of employees belonging to the "bad apples" cluster.

HR data include the seniority in the banking institution and the type of job held (trader or sales), but also the end-of-year performance ratings and the bonus, since both traders and sales are bonusable employees. To consider links between personality traits and conduct performance, the 14 members of the "bad apples" cluster were asked to take a Big Five test. They were informed that their responses would be kept in absolute confidence. The five-factor model, or Big Five test, is currently the most widely accepted theory of personality traits.[7] The Big Five factor markers are: (1) openness; (2) conscientiousness; (3) extraversion; (4) agreeableness; (5) neuroticism. The five dimensions of the Big Five model are best understood as containing a bundle of traits. Sanjay Srivastava, a social psychologist from the University of Oregon, suggests the following:

- *Openness.* Includes traits like having wide interests and being imaginative and insightful.
- *Conscientiousness.* Includes traits like being organized, thorough and planful.
- *Extraversion.* The broad dimension of extraversion encompasses such specific traits as being talkative, energetic and assertive.
- *Agreeableness.* Includes traits like being sympathetic, kind and affectionate.
- *Neuroticism.* Includes traits like being tense, moody and anxious.

We use a public-domain 50-item IPIP (International Personality Item Pool) of the Big Five markers developed by Serge Helfrich (available at https://personality.sergehelfrich.eu/). See the IPIP website (http://ipip.ori.org/) for further details. This psychometric survey is reproduced in **Appendix 3**.

Lastly, we compile data on the business activities of risk-takers, including their department/desk and the type of activities they operate in (see **Figure 38**). Three types of trading activities are considered: market making, proprietary trading and agency. The Securities and Exchange Commission (SEC) defines a market-maker as *"a firm that stands ready to buy or sell a stock at public quoted prices"*.[8] Market-makers must publish a price and amount that they are willing to buy or sell throughout the trading day. Proprietary trading is when a financial institution trades for direct gain instead of commission. Essentially, the institution has decided to profit from the market rather than from commissions from processing trades.[9] Some traders act as "execution-only" traders, meaning they ensure a client's trade executes as per their instructions. These trades are known as agency trades, as the trader is acting as an agent for their client, and simply following their instructions.[10]

The results of this root-cause analysis highlight some revealing characteristics shared by risk-takers in the "bad apples" cluster (see **Figure 39**).

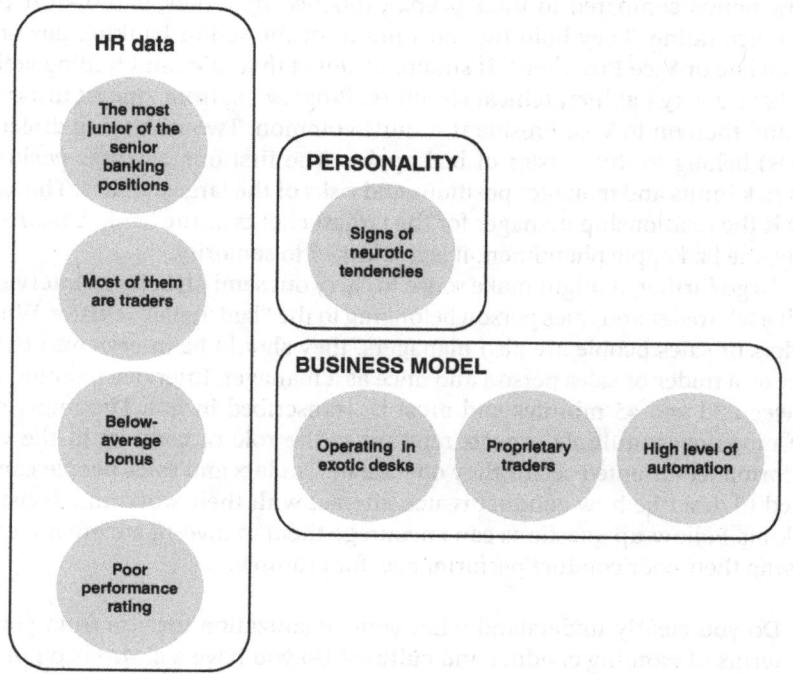

FIGURE 39   Main traits of bad apples

They perform fairly complex trading activities on exotic products and use a variety of complex trading strategies to achieve their goals, such as high-frequency algorithmic trading (HFT). They are proprietary traders and are thus exposed to more market risk than agency traders, who do not take any risk since they are not exposed to any market volatility. As proprietary traders, their sole objective is to generate as a high a profit as possible by taking advantage of short-term fluctuations in the market. This is obviously a risky business.

The observed high level of automation is due to the use of HFT, a subset of algorithmic trading.[11] Frequent small trades executed in milliseconds for very short-term investment horizons do not prevent conduct breaches. Algorithmic trading frauds are also possible. Traders can develop algorithms that run amok when certain conditions are in place. There is a temptation that someone will use the mathematical formulas to improve proprietary trading.

Most traders in the "bad apples" cluster seem to have some type of neurotic personality—according to the Big Five test. Given the low cluster size (14 people), calculating a percentage is not significant. Contrary to common wisdom that traders share a certain set of personality traits (e.g., aggressiveness, extraversion or neuroticism), some studies found evidence of little correlation between personality traits and trading performance.[12]

From the HR data in **Figure 39**, we learn that the 14 bad apples receive a low bonus compared to their peers, explained by a poor end-of-year performance rating. They hold the most junior of the senior banking positions (Associate or Vice President). It should be noted that sales and trading activities have a very flat hierarchical structure. Progressing from analyst to associate and then on to Vice President is quite common. Two managing directors (MDs) belong to this cluster of bad apples. The first one oversees positions and risk limits and manages positions and risks of the largest trades. The sales MD is the relationship manager for the largest clients of the bank. Unsurprisingly, the bad apple phenomenon is not linked to seniority.

To go further, it might make sense to carry out semi-structured interviews with each trader and sales person belonging to the "bad apples" cluster. Where traders or sales people are also managers, they should be interviewed twice, once as a trader or sales person and once as a manager. Interviews should last between 30 and 45 minutes and must be transcribed in full. The interviews can range over multiple aspects relevant to the role of conduct in the very performance-oriented sector they operate in. Traders and sales people can be asked to describe how conduct issues interact with their work and decision-making. Follow-up questions can encourage them to investigate other factors driving their poor conduct performance, for example:

- Do you clearly understand what your organization expects from you in terms of banking conduct and culture? Do you have a clear vision of the level of tolerance in risks that is acceptable?

This is a great paradox for risk-takers to be incentivized to generate (very) short-term results at the expense of client and bank interests. When the tone from the top leads risk-takers to compromise their integrity and behaviour, it becomes difficult to create the conduct culture when they have skin in the game. Behind a "bad apple" there is often a "bad barrel".

- Do you think your leadership is overly dominant? Can you really question or challenge decisions openly, or must you follow the example from the top?
  "Where a culture is open and staff are able to speak up, decision-making is enhanced and risks are flagged" says Andrew Bailey, former CEO of the Financial Conduct Authority (FCA).[13] When the organization is not open-minded because it holds the absolute truth and no other vision can be relevant, it is a starting point for tolerating misconduct.

PUTTING A TANGIBLE VALUE ON DIVERSITY AND INCLUSIVENESS

In our root-cause analysis of the "bad apples" cluster, we have not included an important factor called diversity. Yet, fostering diversity and inclusion can contribute to changing the behaviour of those risk-takers for the better. Diversity and inclusion are central because they result in better judgement and better decision-making—two drivers of better conduct and behaviour.

It is widely acknowledged that diversity and inclusiveness are two inter-related concepts. However, there is no definitive answer about how to measure them. There is a plethora of metrics, indicators or tools—quantitative or qualitative—available everywhere. To alleviate the selection problem, we suggest using non-confidential HR data because they are relatively easy to collect.

In what follows, we select the following data about the 14 risk-takers identified as bad apples:

- Gender: man/woman
- Marital status: married/divorced/single
- Children: no children/1 to 3 children/more than 3 children
- Background: scientific/non-scientific

These criteria are easily customizable depending on both the objective and needs of the user. Here, the emphasis is put on the measure of diversity using the above data because it is implementable. Ideally speaking, the practice of diversity should be seen in terms of people, backgrounds and experience, opinions and thinking, and much more. Unfortunately, most of these items are difficult to use as inputs when it comes to measuring diversity through a quantitative indicator.

To measure diversity within the cluster of bad apples, we use the Shannon index of diversity.[14] The Shannon diversity index is an information statistic index widely used in the fields of biodiversity and ecological monitoring. A diversity index is a mathematical measure of species diversity in a particular community. Denoted H, the index is calculated as follows:

$$\text{Shannon index } (H) = -\sum_{i=1}^{s} p_i \ln p_i$$

In the Shannon index, p is the proportion (n/N) of individuals of one particular species (n) over the total number of individuals (N), ln is the natural logarithm, Σ is the sum of calculation and s is the number of species. Interpretating the Shannon index is straightforward: the higher the value of H, the higher the diversity of species in a given community. When $H = 0$, this means a community that has only one species.

The detailed calculation of the Shannon index of diversity for the cluster of bad apples is displayed in **Table 35**. This cluster of 14 people defines the community and the column headed "description" corresponds to the "species". **Table 35** can be quickly reproduced in an Excel spreadsheet. For the natural logarithm, select the Math and Trigo functions and then select the LN function which returns the natural logarithm of a number.

s (number of species) = 10

N (total number of individuals) = 56

$\sum p_i \ln p_i = -2.151$

$H = -(-0.189 + -0.260 + -0.157 + \ldots + -0.119) = 2.151$

TABLE 35   Calculation of the Shannon index of diversity

Item	Description	Number of Individuals (n)	n/N	p_i	$\ln p_i$	$p_i \ln p_i$
Marital status	Married	4	4/56	0.071	−2.639	−0.189
	Divorced	7	7/56	0.125	−2.079	−0.260
	Single	3	3/56	0.054	−2.927	−0.157
Children	No children	5	5/56	0.089	−2.416	−0.216
	1 to 3 children	5	5/56	0.089	−2.416	−0.216
	More than 3 children	4	4/56	0.071	−2.639	−0.189
Gender	Man	3	3/56	0.054	−2.927	−0.157
	Woman	11	11/56	0.196	−1.627	−0.320
Background	Scientific	12	12/56	0.241	−1.540	−0.330
	Non-scientific	2	2/56	0.036	−3.332	−0.119
	Total	**56**			H	**2.151**

The Shannon diversity index for the cluster of bad apples is 2.151. There is no upper limit to the index.[15] The maximum value is reached for $\ln(s)$, indicating that all species have the same number of individuals. Here we have $\ln(10) = 2.303$; we can thus conclude that the diversity is high within the cluster/community of bad apples. This high diversity is due to the wide gap between man/woman and scientific/non-scientific backgrounds within this cluster (see **Table 35**).

In a trading room, most employees hold a strong technical background, but often they have trouble balancing the trade-off between their daily business and the potential long-term impacts of their decisions on their clients and firm. More people with a non-scientific profile should be hired by financial institutions. Also, why are there so few women in trading rooms and, more generally speaking, in the field of finance? While women make up more than half of the entry-level finance workforce in the United States, only about 6% of the top public financial institutions have women in senior positions.[16] Diversity and inclusion help to mitigate the danger of groupthink. Including non-quant people and more women is a real opportunity.[17]

NOTES

1. As part of the project, I was responsible for developing the conduct risk index presented in this book in a slightly different version and everything dealing with data analytics. For confidentiality reasons, neither the name of the bank nor the dataset can be disclosed.
2. Technically speaking, we use a finite mixture model for the cluster analysis. Due to their high flexibility, mixture models are gaining momentum in a variety of fields— astronomy, biology, genetics, economics, engineering and marketing, for example. The interested reader will find a technical presentation of clustering using mixture modelling in Lebret *et al.* (2015).
3. BIC: Bayesian Information Criterion (also known as Schwarz Criterion).
4. When no ex-ante information about the number of groups is available, Hamparsum Bozdogan, a professor of business analytics and statistics from the University of Tennessee, recommends varying it between 1 and the smallest integer larger than $n^{0.3}$ (where n is the number of observations). In our example, with 157 risk-takers, we have $157^{0.3} = 4.55$. The smallest integer larger than 4.55 is 5, meaning that we should try an n-group solution ($n = 1,\ldots,5$) and then use the BIC to select the best.
5. From regulation to results: Bank strategy. *The Banker*, Special Report, January 2015.
6. The term "rolling bad apples" denotes individuals who engage in misconduct but are able to obtain subsequent employment elsewhere without disclosing their earlier misconduct to the new employer. It may also apply to individuals who engage in misconduct, change roles within the same firm and continue engaging in misconduct (Source: FSB, 2018).

7. These five scales have been developed by Lewis R. Goldberg, Professor Emeritus at the University of Oregon. For interested readers, see Goldberg (1992).
8. Source: https://www.sec.gov/pdf/nasd1/systems.pdf
9. Source: https://www.bis.org/statistics/glossary.htm
10. Working on the trading desk, *FMI Online*, 25 November 2020. More available at https://fmi.online/working-on-the-trading-desk-2/?v=11aedd0e4327
11. Automated transactions where a computer algorithm decides the order of submission and execution with little or no human intervention. According to Select USA (the US government programme led by the U.S. Department of Commerce), about 60–75% of overall trading volume in the US equity market, European financial markets and major Asian capital markets is generated through algorithmic trading.
12. See, e.g., Lo et al. (2005).
13. *Culture in financial institutions: It's everywhere and nowhere.* Speech by Andrew Bailey, Chief Executive Officer of the FCA, at the HKMA Annual Conference for Independent Non-Executive Directors. Last updated 20 March 2017. Available at https://www.fca.org.uk/news/speeches/culture-financial-institutions-everywhere-nowhere
14. Weaver (1949).
15. Generally speaking, and regardless of the community under review, the Shannon index ranges from less than 1 to 4.5, but rarely more. A value close to $H = 0.5$ is very low.
16. Source: *Why are there so few women in finance? 9 Remarkable stats.* Quantic blog, 5 August 2022. Available at https://quantic.edu/blog/2022/08/05/why-are-there-so-few-women-in-finance-9-remarkable-stats/
17. A "quant" is a *person* who relies on statistical and mathematical methods/models to do his job – mainly speaking, a financial engineer.

Appendix

APPENDIX 1

2022 List of Global Systemically Important Banks (G-SIBs)

As of 21 November 2022 (in alphabetical order)
Source: Financial Stability Board (FSB). https://www.fsb.org/

1. Agricultural Bank of China
2. Bank of America
3. Bank of China
4. Bank of New York Mellon
5. Barclays
6. BNP Paribas
7. China Construction Bank
8. Citigroup
9. Credit Suisse
10. Deutsche Bank
11. Goldman Sachs
12. Groupe BPCE
13. Groupe Crédit Agricole
14. HSBC
15. Industrial and Commercial Bank of China
16. ING
17. JP Morgan Chase
18. Mitsubishi UFJ FG
19. Mizuho FG
20. Morgan Stanley
21. Royal Bank of Canada
22. Santander
23. Société Générale
24. Standard Chartered
25. State Street
26. Sumitomo Mitsui FG
27. Toronto Dominion

28. UBS
29. UniCredit
30. Wells Fargo

APPENDIX 2

Combined List of FCA and PRA Senior Management Functions (SMFs)

SMF	Description	FCA function	PRA function
SMF1	Chief Executive		✓
SMF2	Chief Finance function		✓
SMF3	Executive Director	✓	
SMF4	Chief Risk function		✓
SMF5	Head of Internal Audit function		✓
SMF6	Head of Key Business Area function		✓
SMF7	Group Entity Senior Manager function		✓
SMF9	Chairman function		✓
SMF10	Chair of the Risk Committee		✓
SMF11	Chair of the Audit Committee		✓
SMF12	Chair of the Remuneration Committee		✓
SMF13	Chair of the Nominations Committee	✓	
SMF14	Senior Independent Director		✓
SMF15[a]	Chair of the With-Profits Committee	✓	
SMF16	Compliance Oversight function	✓	
SMF17	Money Laundering Reporting function	✓	
SMF18	Other Overall Responsibility function	✓	
SMF19	Head of Third-Country Branch		✓
SMF20	Chief Actuary function		✓
SMF20a	With-Profits Actuary function		✓
SMF21	EEA Branch Senior Manager	✓	
SMF22	Other Local Responsibility	✓	
SMF23	Chief Underwriting Officer		✓

SMF	Description	FCA function	PRA function
SMF23a	Underwriting Risk Oversight function (Lloyds)		✓
SMF23b	Conduct Risk Oversight function (Lloyds)	✓	
SMF24	Chief Operations function		✓
SMF27	Partner function	✓	

ªIncludes any person(s) performing the With-Profits advisory arrangement.
FCA: Financial Conduct Authority
PRA: Prudential Regulation Authority

APPENDIX 3

Big Five Personality Test: 50-Item IPIP Version of the Big Five Markers

Indicate for each statement whether it is (1) very inaccurate; (2) moderately inaccurate; (3) neither accurate nor inaccurate; (4) moderately accurate; or (5) very accurate as a description of you.

	Very Inaccurate	Moderately Inaccurate	Neither Accurate nor Inaccurate	Moderately Accurate	Very Accurate
1. Am the life of the party	O	O	O	O	O
2. Feel little concern for others	O	O	O	O	O
3. Am always prepared	O	O	O	O	O
4. Get stressed out easily	O	O	O	O	O
5. Have a rich vocabulary	O	O	O	O	O
6. Don't talk a lot	O	O	O	O	O
7. Am interested in people	O	O	O	O	O

(*continued*)

	Very Inaccurate	Moderately Inaccurate	Neither Accurate nor Inaccurate	Moderately Accurate	Very Accurate
8. Leave my belongings around	○	○	○	○	○
9. Am relaxed most of the time	○	○	○	○	○
10. Have difficulty understanding abstract ideas	○	○	○	○	○
11. Feel comfortable around people	○	○	○	○	○
12. Insult people	○	○	○	○	○
13. Pay attention to details	○	○	○	○	○
14. Worry about things	○	○	○	○	○
15. Have a vivid imagination	○	○	○	○	○
16. Keep in the background	○	○	○	○	○
17. Sympathize with others' feelings	○	○	○	○	○
18. Make a mess of things	○	○	○	○	○
19. Seldom feel blue	○	○	○	○	○
20. Am not interested in abstract ideas	○	○	○	○	○
21. Start conversations	○	○	○	○	○

	Very Inaccurate	Moderately Inaccurate	Neither Accurate nor Inaccurate	Moderately Accurate	Very Accurate
22. Am not interested in other people's problems	O	O	O	O	O
23. Get chores done right away	O	O	O	O	O
24. Am easily disturbed	O	O	O	O	O
25. Have excellent ideas	O	O	O	O	O
26. Have little to say	O	O	O	O	O
27. Have a soft heart	O	O	O	O	O
28. Often forget to put things back in their proper place	O	O	O	O	O
29. Get upset easily	O	O	O	O	O
30. Do not have a good imagination	O	O	O	O	O
31. Talk to a lot of different people at parties	O	O	O	O	O
32. Am not really interested in others	O	O	O	O	O
33. Like order	O	O	O	O	O

(continued)

	Very Inaccurate	Moderately Inaccurate	Neither Accurate nor Inaccurate	Moderately Accurate	Very Accurate
34. Change my mood a lot	○	○	○	○	○
35. Am quick to understand things	○	○	○	○	○
36. Don't like to draw attention to myself	○	○	○	○	○
37. Take time out for others	○	○	○	○	○
38. Shirk my duties	○	○	○	○	○
39. Have frequent mood swings	○	○	○	○	○
40. Use difficult words	○	○	○	○	○
41. Don't mind being the centre of attention	○	○	○	○	○
42. Feel others' emotions	○	○	○	○	○
43. Follow a schedule	○	○	○	○	○
44. Get irritated easily	○	○	○	○	○
45. Spend time reflecting on things	○	○	○	○	○
46. Am quiet around strangers	○	○	○	○	○
47. Make people feel at ease	○	○	○	○	○

	Very Inaccurate	Moderately Inaccurate	Neither Accurate nor Inaccurate	Moderately Accurate	Very Accurate
48. Am exacting in my work	○	○	○	○	○
49. Often feel blue	○	○	○	○	○
50. Am full of ideas	○	○	○	○	○

References

Anderson, A. (2013). *Business Statistics for Dummies*. Wiley.

BCBS (1988). *International convergence of capital measurement and capital standards*, July.

BCBS (1996). *Amendment to the capital accord to incorporate market risks*, January.

BCBS (2006). *International convergence of capital measurement and capital standards: A revised framework* (comprehensive version), June.

BCBS (2009). *Revisions to the Basel II market risk framework*, July.

BCBS (2010). *Basel III: A global regulatory framework for more resilient banks and banking systems*, December.

BCBS (2014a). *Basel III: The net stable funding ratio*, October.

BCBS (2014b). *Basel III leverage ratio framework and disclosure requirements*, January.

BCBS (2019a). *Minimum capital requirements for market risk*, January (revised February).

BCBS (2019b). *Explanatory note on the minimum capital requirements for market risk*, January.

BCBS (2021). *Principles for the effective management and supervision of climate-related financial risks*. Consultative Document, November.

BCBS (2023). *OPE calculation of RWA for operational risk, OPE25 Standardised approach* (version effective as of 1 January 2023).

Bollerslev, T. (1986). Generalized autoregressive conditional heteroskedasticity. *Journal of Econometrics*, 31(3), pp. 307–327.

FCA (2019). *The Senior Managers and Certification Regime: Guide for FCA Solo-Regulated Firms*, July.

FSB (2018). *Strengthening Governance Frameworks to Mitigate Misconduct Risk: A Toolkit for Firms and Supervisors*, 20 April.

Goldberg, L. R. (1992). The development of markers for the Big-Five factor structure. *Psychological Assessment*, 4, pp. 26–42.

Gumbel, E. J. (1958). *Statistics of Extremes*. Columbia University Press.

Hsu, A., Johnson, L. A. and Lloyd, A. (2013). *Measuring Progress: A Practical Guide from the Developers of the Environmental Performance Index (EPI)*. Yale Center for Environmental Law & Policy.

Lebret, R., Iovleff, S., Langrognet, F., Biernacki, C., Celeux, G. and Govaert, G. (2015). Rmixmod: The R package of the model-based unsupervised, supervised, and semi-supervised classification Mixmod library. *Journal of Statistical Software*, 67, pp. 1–29.

Lo, A. W., Repin, D. V. and Steenbarger, B. N. (2005). Fear and greed in financial markets: A clinical study of day-traders. *American Economic Review*, 95(2), pp. 352–359.

Markowitz, H. (1952). Portfolio selection. *Journal of Finance*, 7(1), pp. 77–91.

Nelsen, R. B (2006). *An Introduction to Copulas*, 2nd edn. Springer.

RiskMetrics™ (1996). *Technical Document*, 4th edn. Available at https://www.msci .com/documents/10199/5915b101-4206-4ba0-aee2-3449d5c7e95a

Roncalli, T. (2020). *Handbook of Financial Risk Management*. Chapman & Hall/CRC Press.

Taleb, N. (2007). *The Black Swan: The Impact of the Highly Improbable*. Random House.

Tufano, P. (2003). Financial innovation. In G. M. Constantinides, M. Harris and R. M. Stulz (Eds), *Handbook of the Economics of Finance*, vol. 1, pp. 307–335. North-Holland.

Weaver, W. (1949). The mathematics of communication. *Scientific American*, 181(1), pp. 11–15.

Zimbardo, P. (2011). *The Lucifer Effect: How Good People Turn Evil*. Random House.

Contents

List of Figures

List of Tables

Index